D0957742

STAND STRONG

JUDY JACOBS

Charisma
HOUSE
A STRANG COMPANY

Most STRANG COMMUNICATIONS/CHARISMA HOUSE/SILOAM/FRONTLINE/REALMS products are available at special quantity discounts for bulk purchase for sales promotions, premiums, fund-raising, and educational needs. For details, write Strang Communications/Charisma House/Siloam/ FrontLine/Realms, 600 Rinehart Road, Lake Mary, Florida 32746, or telephone (407) 333-0600.

STAND STRONG by Judy Jacobs
Published by Charisma House
A Strang Company
600 Rinehart Road
Lake Mary, Florida 32746
www.charismahouse.com

Unless otherwise noted, all Scripture quotations are from the King James Version of the Bible.

Scripture quotations marked AMP are from the Amplified Bible, Old Testament copyright © 1965, 1987 by the Zondervan Corporation. The Amplified New Testament copyright © 1954, 1958, 1987 by the Lockman Foundation. Used by permission.

Scripture quotations marked NAS are from the New American Standard Bible. Copyright © 1960, 1962, 1963, 1968, 1971, 1972, 1973, 1975, 1977 by the Lockman Foundation. Used by permission. (www. Lockman.org)

Scripture quotations marked NKJV are from the New King James Version of the Bible. Copyright © 1979, 1980, 1982 by Thomas Nelson, Inc., publishers. Used by permission.

Scripture quotations marked NLT are from the Holy Bible, New Living Translation, copyright © 1996. Used by permission of Tyndale House Publishers, Inc., Wheaton, IL 60189.

Scripture quotations marked NRSV are from the New Revised Standard Version of the Bible. Copyright © 1989 by the Division of Christian Education of the National Council of the Churches of Christ in the USA. Used by permission.

Scripture quotations marked RSV are from the Revised Standard Version of the Bible. Copyright © 1946, 1952, 1971 by the Division of Christian Education of the National Council of the Churches of Christ in the USA. Used by permission.

Scripture quotations marked THE MESSAGE are from *The Message: The Bible in Contemporary English*, copyright © 1993, 1994, 1995, 1996, 2000, 2001, 2002. Used by permission of NavPress Publishing Group.

Scripture quotations marked TLB are from *The Living Bible*. Copyright © 1971. Used by permission of Tyndale House Publishers, Inc., Wheaton, IL 60189.

Cover Designer, Marvin Eans; Design Director, Bill Johnson
Author photographs copyright © 2006 Adrian Wilcox/Aslan Studios, Inc.
All rights reserved. Used by permission.
www.aslan-studios.com

Library of Congress Cataloging-in-Publication Data
Jacobs, Judy, 1957-
Stand strong / Judy Jacobs.
     p. cm.
Includes bibliographical references and index.
ISBN 978-1-59979-066-4   1. Christian life--Biblical teaching. I. Title.
BV4501.3.J328 2007
248.4--dc22

2006037243

07 08 09 10 11 — 9 8 7 6 5 4 3 2
Printed in the United States of America

THIS book *Stand Strong* is lovingly dedicated to my wonderful man of God, Jamie Tuttle. For the last fourteen years of our married life, Jamie has had to "stand strong" in his faith, his confidence, and his love for me, believing in who I was, before who I am now, which Paul says, "By the grace of God I am what I am" (1 Cor. 15:10). Jamie has pushed me with his very loving and gentle hand to believe for the greatest, the highest, and the excellent. I can truly say, "If it had not been, first of all for the Lord on my side..." and then this mighty man of God, I would never have seen all of our dreams come true. Baby, I look forward to tomorrow, because I know that the best is yet to come. (1436)

This book is also dedicated to my beautiful daughters, Kaylee and Erica Tuttle, the joys of my heart. In the midst of your short lives, you have had to "stand strong" in green rooms, guesthouses, hotel rooms, long bus trips, restaurant food, airplane trips, and don't forget, the long sermons that your dad and mommy preach. You are true troopers! We are so proud of you! We love you for your sacrifice, and heaven will reward you for everything!

My love and appreciation go out to our families, the Jacobs family and the Tuttle family, for "standing strong" with us for the past fourteen years and seeing us through with your support, prayers, and encouragement.

My heartfelt thanks go out to two very important families in our lives and ministries who have stood strong with us and have supported our dreams and our vision: Charlie and Kathie Kennemer and Olan and Angela St. John. You are definitely "the wind beneath our wings." We love you, and only He will be able to reward you for your faithfulness.

ACKNOWLEDGMENTS

WITH my heart I would like to say thank you to some very important people in my life:

To Pastor Paula White, my mentor, life coach, and friend, for your unequivocal stance to "stand strong" in front of all of the world and to teach us from example what standing strong looks like.

To Stephen and Joy Strang for this incredibly brilliant opportunity to be able to publish this work that I feel is direct from the throne of God for this time and season in all of our lives.

To the entire Product Development team of Strang Communications, my heartfelt thanks for all of your diligence in making sure that this manuscript is top-notch.

A very special thank you to Kathy Deering for all the work, toil, and sacrifice with this manuscript from the beginning to the end. Your diligence is unheard of.

To Melissa Hill and all of the His Song Ministries staff who have celebrated with us, cried with us, labored with us, but most of all stood strong with us to see this dream come to pass. We love you!

CONTENTS

WOW! Get ready to be blessed and refreshed in your love relationship with God! He must have known the body of Christ needed an awesome and uncompromising message on *getting real* in your faith when He spoke it into His choice vessel Judy Jacobs to bring it on in *Stand Strong*.

Whether you've been walking in the abundance of God your whole life, recently accepted Jesus Christ as your Lord and Savior, or you're somewhere between the two, *Stand Strong* will reveal the true destiny of your union with Him in new ways. Judy has a divinely inspired word for you on getting "violent" in seeking God's kingdom, becoming what she calls a "high-impact" Christian, strategically God-positioned to change the world around you!

You will know how you can nourish and activate your faith by reinvesting every portion of your life in God—drawing on the power of His Holy Spirit to restore you during times of trial, to transform you as you proclaim His name, and to equip you to lead others toward Jesus. You will find yourself being armed "to resist the enemy in the time of evil" during the last days, as Paul encouraged in Ephesians 6:13 (NLT). Get ready to be equipped for victory!

Powerful insights on getting a God-given vision and developing your call are closely examined and revealed. The lives of several "greats"—from King David to modern-day "standers" like Billy Graham—are revealed to determine the godly characteristics found in those who are truly Spirit-filled. This provides a fresh perspective on how you can develop those same traits.

Chapters on the power of persistent prayer and consistent praise and worship reveal the deeper spiritual rewards, blessings, and covering found in these invaluable lines of communication to God. And in the final chapter, "Having Done All," Judy will leave you with an empowering message of God's transformational call for your life as you mature in your faith by "walking obediently" with Him.

Stand Strong will renew and reactivate your passion to discover God's destined journey for your life. Read on, and be blessed by this mighty woman of God with an anointed message!

—Paula White, Senior Pastor
Without Walls International Church

WHEN I finished (so I thought) writing my first book, *Take It By Force!* I realized that it needed one final chapter. I called that chapter "Take a Stand," and in it I described what you should do when you have tried everything and nothing has worked. What do you do when you have done it all? You *stand.*

For that matter, what do you do the whole time you're actively "doing"—praying, fasting, fighting, proclaiming, and so on? You stand.

You stand as tall as you can, with your feet flat on the ground, strong in your faith. You keep your mouth open with praise and your eyes open for God to show you the supernatural. You keep your hands raised to give Him praise. You keep your heart pure.

You don't sit down. You don't lie down. You don't run off anxiously to another prayer meeting. You don't call your mama. You don't dial 911. You just simply *stand.*

Have you ever thought about how much standing goes into a successful walk of faith? As I thought and prayed about it, I found out that standing includes declaring, decreeing, praising, proclaiming, and waiting. As a matter of fact, I found out there's so much to say about how to stand, where to stand, why to stand, when to stand, and what to stand for that a person could write a book about it. So that's what I did, and you're holding that book in your hands.

As you read this, you may be sitting down. Maybe you're lying in your bed at night, reading a few pages before you turn out the light. It could be that you're standing in a bookstore, leafing through the pages to see if you want to buy the book. Regardless of your stance at this moment, I can guarantee you—you won't be able to read very much of *Stand Strong* without starting to feel that something is standing up inside you. You will find yourself standing up taller inside your *spirit*, which is the real you.

I want to motivate you as you have never been motivated before—to *stand strong* in your personal walk of faith in Christ Jesus. I want to show you why to do it and how to do it. I want you to be able to see, as I have, how the concept of standing permeates the Bible and how, chapter by chapter, all of the Christian life is about standing in faith. Are we really going to stay put and keep standing? I want you to grasp the characteristics of your standing stance: having confidence in your calling, achieving strength in your adversities, developing balanced and godly character, learning to use "violent" and active faith, becoming persistent in your prayer, and growing consistent in your praise and worship.

Above all, I want you to stand so strong and so long that you will become an overcomer of the highest caliber. I want you to become mighty in your spirit, unsurprised when your life journey gets rough, unafraid and even joyful in the face of what may seem like a personal defeat or a major disaster.

I want you to be equal to anything, because of Jesus.

—Judy Jacobs

Wherefore take unto you the whole armour of God, that ye may be able to withstand in the evil day, and having done all, to stand.

—EPHESIANS 6:13

This is the true grace of God. Stand firm in it!

—1 PETER 5:12, NAS

CHAPTER I

THE "STANDING STANCE"

CHILDREN love that Sunday school song "Silver and Gold Have I None." Usually the kids start out singing that song sitting down in their little chairs. Then, when they hit the chorus, they jump to their feet so they can act out the *walking* and *leaping* and *praising God* parts. They want to be like the lame man at the gate called Beautiful who was healed (Acts 3:2–8). They are excited to show off what their God can do.

But do you know something? Those same kids, after they grow out of that song, often forget that they belong to a God who can heal. Most of them have healthy, sturdy legs; they are not lame physically. Yet they may never realize that there's a kind of lameness in their *spirits* that needs a healing touch from God just as someone's legs may need physical healing. They may not understand all the different ways faith and grace can work. They may forget that Jesus Christ of Nazareth is still at work to make people whole through and through.

So they just grow up and they sit there. They forget to stand up.

EXCEPTIONAL FAITH

What about you? Have you jumped to your feet in faith? If you did that once, are you still standing?

I want you to be the exception to the norm. I want to birth exceptional faith in your heart. I want you to become a powerful example to others, even possibly a person who can mentor others in the spiritual art of standing strong in faith. I want you to be mighty in your spirit, whole through and through, to be able to stand up in adversity and declare, "I will bless the LORD at all times: his praise shall continually be in my mouth" (Ps. 34:1). I want you to stand so strong in Jesus that you'll be famous for it. I want you to be somebody people will write home about.

Look around you. Think about the people you have known. Can you think of someone who just stands out because he *stands* so well? Unless you live in Antarctica, you should be able to find somebody like that. God always makes sure that He has people who can stand strong, so His kingdom can advance.

Even if you can't think of anybody you know, you can look in your Bible, where you will find more people who stood strong than you can ever list. For example:

David. David got good at standing strong. You can read his life story in the first and second books of Samuel.

When he was just a teenager, he was on his feet already—tending his sheep. He kept doing that for a while after Samuel anointed him king. While he was on that assignment, he grew strong enough to kill wild animals. Then he volunteered to stand against Goliath. He tried on some borrowed armor, but soon found it was too awkward for him. So he took it off, and he went in the power of God's Spirit to stand there before the giant Philistine. Without armor, David looked pretty silly, completely defenseless. Goliath laughed at him and cursed him. But within moments, David was standing in victory over the giant he had just killed with one well-placed rock.

King Saul sent for the young hero. "Let David, I pray thee, *stand* before me; for he hath found favour in my sight" (1 Sam. 16:22, emphasis added). Once he arrived to stand before the king in the house of Saul, young David had to learn to watch for new dangers. More than once he had to dodge the king's murderous rage in order to stay safe. Yet, as he had learned to do when he was tending his father's sheep, he spent much time writing and singing songs of praise to his God. Worship was his faith response to God, and in return, God gave him mighty strength and a strategic mind. Every time he went back out to battle, David stood before his troops in fresh victory. He was anointed and he was appointed, and he kept on standing strong by the power of his God.

David's victories didn't make him too popular with jealous old Saul. In fact, he had to run for his life. He had to travel from one hiding place to another, and it was hard to know who was safe to trust. Remember, this was back in the days when you couldn't just take a bus or a cab to your next destination. All David had for transportation were the two feet he had to stand on. He had to be nimble, humble, and strong. He had to believe that God had a plan for his future. He had to believe that all of this running was worth it.

One day, David and some of his men were hiding in a cave. Saul, who had been in hot pursuit of David, came into the cave, not knowing that they were there. David's men urged him to take advantage of the situation and kill his enemy, but David had stronger character than that. Instead of taking the easy way to freedom by putting an end to Saul, he only snipped off part of Saul's hem. Then he shouted after Saul, showing him what he had done: "May the Lord judge as to which of us is right and punish whichever one of us is guilty. He is my lawyer and defender, and he will rescue me from your power!" (1 Sam. 24:15, TLB). David chose to let God defend him. He stood in confidence that God would save him, and God did.

God also helped David to save others, and he did it against all odds. Remember when the Amalekites raided Ziklag and carried off all of the wives and children of David and his men? David's men were so upset that some of them became like enemies to David for a while. But the Bible says, "David took strength from the Lord" (1 Sam. 30:6, TLB). With the fresh strength he received from God, he raided the Amalekites and recovered everything and everybody that had been stolen.

Even when Saul died and David was installed as king, he had to keep standing in God's power. He couldn't relax his alertness or rest on his achievements. He had no end of trouble from Saul's people and even from his own sons, not to mention the enemies of Israel. The opposition only made him stronger. As the years went by, he became even more famous for his successes on the battlefield. Who had ever seen such a great warrior-king? He could stand up under any kind of pressure, and he kept giving the glory to God.

To celebrate the faithfulness of his God, David wrote these lyrics for a song:

> This God is my strong refuge,
>   and has made my way safe.
> He made my feet like hinds' feet,
>   and set me secure on the heights.
> He trains my hands for war,
>   so that my arms can bend a bow of bronze.
> Thou hast given me the shield of thy salvation,
>   and thy help made me great.
> Thou didst give a wide place for my steps under me,
>   and my feet did not slip.
>
> —2 SAMUEL 22:33–37, RSV

Without a doubt, David is one of the most long-standing, strong-standing men God ever had on this earth.

Deborah. As a female gospel singer myself, I like the fact that another female singer was Deborah, who the Bible says was also a prophetess and a respected judge (which was very unusual, since she was a woman). When evil forces were assembled against Israel under the command of Sisera, Deborah definitely stood firm on behalf of Israel. Even Barak, a commander of ten thousand men, didn't dare go into a battle that the Lord had commanded him to fight unless Deborah would agree to accompany him. She carried much more of the Lord's anointing than he did, and he knew it.

> Barak said unto her, If thou wilt go with me, then I will go: but if thou wilt not go with me, then I will not go. And she said, I will surely go with thee: notwithstanding the journey that thou takest shall not be for thine honour; for the LORD shall sell Sisera into the hand of a woman. And Deborah arose, and went with Barak to Kedesh.
>
> —JUDGES 4:8–9

It's as if Barak, who must have been in the prime of his life and as strong and skilled as a warrior as any other man, knew he couldn't prevail against the Canaanites unless he had extra support. Barak's "standing stance" depended on the Lord's strength, given to him through a woman.

So what happened? Barak, accompanied by Deborah, summoned his ten thousand men. Coming down from the slopes of Mount Tabor, they attacked the Canaanite forces on the plain of Jezreel, and, in spite of Sisera's dreaded iron chariots (nine hundred of them!), Barak's forces prevailed.

However, Sisera himself escaped on foot. He took refuge in the tent of Jael—a woman who turned out to display every bit as much courage and determination as Deborah. Remember how sweetly Jael invited Israel's enemy inside?

"And Jael went out to meet Sisera, and said unto him, Turn in, my lord, turn in to me; fear not. And when he had turned in unto her into the tent, she covered him with a mantle" (Judg. 4:18). She gave him some goat's milk to drink, and he went to sleep, exhausted. Then the woman did something that nobody would have expected. She was accustomed to setting up her tent as her nomad husband moved the family from place to place. So she simply fetched an extra tent peg and a peg hammer, and then she:

> ... went softly unto him, and smote the nail into his temples, and fastened it into the ground: for he was fast asleep and weary. So he died. And, behold, as Barak pursued Sisera, Jael came out to meet him, and said unto him, Come, and I will shew thee the man whom thou seekest. And when he came into her tent, behold, Sisera lay dead, and the nail was in his temples. So God subdued on that day Jabin the king of Canaan before the children of Israel.
>
> —JUDGES 4:21–23

Deborah sang a song of triumph in which she reminded the people about how dire their circumstances had been before the Lord had turned the battle. She sang about how the villagers had fled to walled cities for protection, leaving the roads and towns empty. Now they could return home in safety and under God's favor because of the mighty victory that had been won for them. Israel had been in a terrible situation, and now they were delivered—by ten thousand soldiers and by the two women who had stood so strong!

After this, the nation of Israel enjoyed forty years of peace and prosperity, and Deborah just kept on standing strong as a wife, wise judge, and capable counselor until the day she died.

Daniel. You've known the story of Daniel and the lions' den since you were a little kid. This handsome young Jewish man had been taken into exile, and he determined to stand strong in his faith regardless of his circumstances. He wouldn't ea[t] food, and he kept to his normal prayer schedule, c[ontinued] loud prayer times even after praying became ille[gal.] caught praying, he was thrown to the lions. You[...] pened next.

The Bible says, "Very early the next morning [the king] hurried out to the lions' den and called out in anguish, 'O Daniel, servant of the Living God, was your God, whom you worship continually, able to deliver you from the lions?'" (Dan. 6:19–20, TLB). Daniel, who probably hadn't even missed his normal prayer times while he was in there, did not have one scratch on him from the ravenous beasts. He was perfectly fine, which is more than you can say for his accusers, who were next in the lions' cafeteria line.

Besides demonstrating a powerful determination to remain true to his God in a pagan society, a few chapters later Daniel also gives us a picture of how to stand in persistent prayer. We read in chapter 10 about how he prayed constantly for three weeks, with no clue about the success or failure of his prayers, deeply burdened with the matter at hand. My friend Myles Munroe writes about Daniel's persistence:

> What did Daniel do? He kept praying. After twenty-one days, an angel arrived with the answer. The point is, Daniel didn't say, "Well, it's been ten days now. This thing doesn't work. I'm going back to doing what I had been doing." No. Daniel believed that if God said something, it was supposed to happen. He wasn't going to stop praying until it was manifested. He was going to persevere until he saw it with his own eyes.[1]

At the end of twenty-one days, Daniel had a surprising heavenly visitation. Daniel reported that the heavenly visitor spoke and "said unto me, O Daniel, a man greatly beloved, understand the words that I speak unto thee, and stand upright: for unto thee am I now sent" (Dan. 10:11). So Daniel, who had "stood" in prayer the whole time without giving up, now stood upright and heard about the results of his prayer.

Daniel kept his standing stance—whether he was on his feet or on his face.

Shadrach, Meshach, and Abednego. Daniel had three friends, Shadrach, Meshach, and Abednego, who were also from Judah. Like Daniel, they were men of God who refused to bow their knee to any god except the true God. As a "reward" for taking a stand and refusing to compromise their beliefs, Nebuchadnezzar had them thrown into the fiery furnace.

You know this story, too. Like Daniel earlier, they came out unscathed—they didn't even smell like smoke, and not one hair had been singed—even though their guards had perished from the fierceness of the flames the minute they cast the three men in.

Now, this story is so familiar to us that we almost forget that those guys did not *know* that they were going to be delivered. They stood strong anyway. They said, "Our God whom we serve is able to deliver us from the furnace of blazing fire; and He will deliver us out of your hand, O king. But even if He does not, let it be known to you, O king, that we are not going to serve your gods or worship the golden image that you have set up" (Dan. 3:17–18, NAS). That's some kind of standing stance!

Gideon. Gideon stood strong (after a little persuasion from God). We read about him in the sixth and seventh chapters of the Book of Judges. The angel of the Lord said to Gideon, "Gideon, the Lord is with you, O valiant warrior. Go and destroy the enemies of God. "

Gideon objected. He said, "You can't expect me to do that. I'm from the tribe of Manasseh. I'm the least of the least. I am a nobody. I am a nothing. I can't destroy the enemies of God." (Have you ever said anything like this? "God, don't send me. Nobody knows me."

"I am unemployed." "I am a single mom." "I am a single adult." "I am a youth." "I can't even speak correctly.")

But the Bible says that the angel of the Lord would not let him go. He kept coming after him even though Gideon felt like the shakiest gun in the west. The angel provoked him and provoked him. Eventually Gideon went to battle. He had God's strength. And you know what? He won.

God breathed His strength into him and called him a "mighty man of valor." It wasn't about puny little Gideon anymore. Now it was about the God *in* him. That's what made him strong enough to battle and to prevail.

Jesus. More than anybody, Jesus stood strong. He could have checked out of His assignment anytime He wanted to, even right up until the last day of His earthly life. He said, "Do you think that I cannot appeal to my Father, and he will at once send me more than twelve legions of angels?" (Matt. 26:53, NRSV). But He didn't do that. He stayed His course.

It was so hard that He sweat blood through His pores in the Garden of Gethsemane. It was so hard that He fell facedown and cried out, "My Father! If it is possible, let this cup be taken away from me. But I want your will, not mine" (Matt. 26:39, TLB). He was arrested, flogged, and hounded through the streets of Jerusalem and nailed to a cross. As He hung there, He cried out, "It is finished," and then they laid His lifeless corpse in a tomb.

Even after that, He *stood back up!* Jesus rose from the dead, and He stood back up! He went down to the corridors of hell, and He took the keys of death, hell, and the grave from the devil and gave them to us. Jesus said, "I will give *you* the keys of the kingdom of heaven; whatever *you* bind on earth will be bound in heaven, and whatever *you* loose on earth will be loosed in heaven" (Matt. 16:19, NIV, emphasis added). The devil does not have any way to get those keys back from Jesus or us, unless we give up on our stand of faith and give them to him.

Today Jesus Christ reigns supremely. He gives each and every one of us who believe in Him the same power that was in Him—to stand against the powers of darkness and, having done all, to stand eternally with Him.

The Standing Stance Today

Brother Andrew. The standing stance becomes habitual after you've been practicing it for a while. You will see what I mean when you look at the lives of the older saints you know about. Take Andrew van der Bijl, for instance, the Dutch evangelist who is better known as Brother Andrew, or "God's Smuggler."

Brother Andrew started out poorly. When he was a young man, he was advised never to travel because of chronic back pain. Feeling the call of God to take Bibles to closed countries, he ignored that medical advice and later got healed in the process of pursuing almost continuous travel. Fifty years later, he is still in good health and still traveling, and nobody knows how many Bibles have been distributed by him and his Open Doors With Brother Andrew organization.

He tells people that he has never been afraid. "There really is no danger, unless you are living your own life," he explains.[2] In other words, if you've given your life to God, as Brother Andrew has, you don't have to worry about it. All you have to do is obey His voice.

People ask him if he would do it all over again. His answer is surprising. "No, it's too big and too much responsibility."[3] But he's quick to add that since God shows up only one step at a time, all he would need to do would be to obey that one step. "One step we can take. If we do that, then the Lord sees how we land on one foot, then the other. If you accept responsibility and grow spiritually, then God will show you the next step."[4]

Darlene Bishop. One of my favorite pastors in the entire world is Darlene Bishop. With her husband, she pastors one of the fastest-growing churches in America. Pastor Darlene has a remarkable testimony of standing strong in faith. In 1986, she had been preaching a series of messages on faith, and God was working mighty miracles. Obviously, the devil didn't like it. One night as she was lying in her bed, she plainly heard the enemy begin to talk to her. In her own words, she tells the story:

> I heard a voice that said, "If you don't stop, I'm going to kill you."
>
> It was so real that I responded immediately. "Devil, you're not big enough!"
>
> "Well, feel your right breast," he urged.
>
> I had just bathed, and I knew that there was nothing there, but now the first spot I touched on my right breast was sore. As I examined myself a little more, I quickly found a lump in that breast the size of a silver dollar.[5]

At that moment, Pastor Darlene's faith was shattered. She cried out to God, "Why me? Don't You know how faithful I have been?" Then she realized that she should stop complaining and start confessing her faith in Him. She remembered how God had performed miracles in her and her family's life before, and she knew that He could do it again.

With newfound faith, she boldly went into her bathroom and proclaimed, "Devil, get out your little black book and write this down. I don't want you to ever forget what God's going to do for me. I'm going to show you that the Word of God that I have been preaching is the same Word that I stand on and live by. God is going to heal me, and there will be no other acceptable outcome to this situation."[6]

As the days, weeks, and months went by, the pain became excruciating, and her breast began to bleed to the extent that she had to wear protective, absorbent pads like breast-feeding mothers wear. She believed in the Word that said, "If any two of you shall agree...," so she selected seven godly women who were intercessors in her church, and they would meet for prayer every day, believing God for a miracle.

This went on for five long and gruesome months. At the end of the fifth month, one night she bled so badly that it soaked right down to her mattress. Again, in her own words:

> This had gone on for five months, and no end was in sight. I stood there at the sink with tears splashing down into the bloody water, and I said, "God, even if the breast rots and falls off into this water, I am still going to preach that You are Jehovah-Rophe, the Lord who heals me. What's going on in this body doesn't change the fact that You are still the Healer. I will believe it and preach it until the very last breath leaves my body."
>
> In that instant, I heard God call my name. If I have ever heard the audible voice of the Lord, it was that day.
>
> "Darlene," He said.
>
> I raised my head. "Yes, Lord."
>
> He said, "Because you have not leaned on the arm of the flesh but have continued to trust in My Word, and because you have continued to confess in the face of the bleeding and the pain that I am your Healer, as of this day you are healed. Go and proclaim it."
>
> And I was healed. The bleeding and the pain stopped instantly, within three days the breast returned to normal, and I have been well since then.[7]

Gaynell Jacobs. When someone asks me for an example of a modern-day person who knew how to stand strong in the faith, the first person I think of is Gaynell Chavis Jacobs, my mom, who is now in heaven. She was the daughter of a Baptist deacon's daughter, who through the influence of her mom ("Grandma Lonnie," to me) was baptized with the power of the Holy Spirit and went on to bring up twelve children to know the Lord and to love and serve the Lord. My mom was a prayer warrior extraordinaire. She would lay hands on the sick, and they would be healed. She was a very unassuming, modest, and unpretentious woman of God, yet she stood strong through everything. She never gave up, and she never let her children give up either.

Joni Eareckson Tada. One modern-day "stander" can't physically stand on her legs right now, because she's wheelchair-bound. I'm talking about Joni Eareckson Tada.

In 1967, seventeen-year-old Joni dove headfirst into some shallow water, and in that instant she became a quadriplegic. Her life since then has been far from easy, and yet she has, with God's abundant help, managed to become a more productive citizen of the kingdom of God than she probably would have if the accident had never occurred. She has founded and expanded a remarkable ministry for the disabled called "Joni and Friends." She has made countless speeches across the United States and in over forty-one countries. Joni has written more than thirty-five books and has executed numerous paintings and drawings by holding a brush or a pencil in her mouth. Her husband, Ken, whom she married in 1982, has managed to combine his own teaching career with caregiving to enable his wife to do all that she does.

In one of her books, Joni writes about the stance of the early Christians, which she always tries to emulate:

> It was said of the early Christians, "You eagerly wait for our *Lord Jesus Christ* to be revealed" (1 Corinthians 1:7). They likened themselves to soldiers poised on the watchtower, workers hoeing for the harvest, athletes straining toward the

finish line, and virgins waiting and watching at night, lamps trimmed, hearts afire, and eyes scanning the horizon for someone special.

The world was no party. They were waiting for the party.

It was clear to them that although the King had begun to set up his kingdom, he hadn't finished. Jesus himself asked his father, "May Thy kingdom come...as it is in *heaven*. He had begun to reverse the effects of sin and its results—pain, death, and disease—but it was just that, a beginning. When the Savior ascended to heaven, no lambs were muzzling lions yet, no swords were being beaten into plowshares...the eyes of all the blind weren't opened yet, the ears of the deaf weren't unstopped, and most of the lame were a far cry from leaping like deer.[8]

One day Joni will leap like a deer, and so will you and I. In the meantime, we need to keep standing in God's grace, walking with upright lives and "pant[ing] for the water brooks" as deer do (Ps. 42:1, NKJV), and bringing as many people with us to heaven as we can possibly bring.

KEEP STANDING STRONG!

Because my mom is in heaven, I can't see her anymore, but I know she's cheering me on as I go through my life. None of us can see them, but surrounding us every minute is a great "cloud of witnesses" (Heb. 12:1), saints who stood firm while they were alive on Earth and who now cheer us on as we persevere through hardships and trials.

We don't always appreciate the idea of being cheered on. Sometimes we would rather hear somebody say, "Well, you did your best. You turned yourself inside out to make your marriage successful, and it's still not working. So go ahead and get a divorce." Or, "You worked your fingers to the bone to provide for those children of yours, and they still went their rebellious way, so just write them off." Or, "You thought tithing your money and giving it to the poor would solve your financial problems, but it didn't. So go ahead and hoard your money and hope for the best."

Don't listen to advice like that! Just keep on praying, keep on tithing, keep on working, keep on hoping, and keep on loving. Keep on growing, keep on praising God, keep on believing, and above all—*keep on standing strong!*

They are brought down and fallen: but we are risen, and stand upright.

—Psalm 20:8

Use every piece of God's armor to resist the enemy in the time of evil, so that after the battle you will still be standing firm. Stand your ground, putting on the sturdy belt of truth and the body armor of God's righteousness. For shoes, put on the peace that comes from the Good News, so that you will be fully prepared. In every battle you will need faith as your shield to stop the fiery arrows aimed at you by Satan. Put on salvation as your helmet, and take the sword of the Spirit, which is the word of God.

—Ephesians 6:13–17, nlt

CHAPTER 2

WHAT DOES IT MEAN TO
STAND STRONG?

STANDING strong depends on more than how sturdy your legs are. Standing strong means you are *strong in your spirit.*

When you are strong in your spirit, you can stand tall (with confidence) and stand long (with perseverance), because you're drawing from a core of strength in your spirit. You have a full reservoir of spiritual strength that comes from God.

Don't get confused about it—your inner strength is *not* the same as being a tough person, someone who has been hardened by life experiences. To stand strong, you do not (necessarily) need a degree from the School of Hard Knocks. You don't stand strong in the way I'm talking about just because you have German, African, or Native American heritage. It's not because you happened to grow up in New York City or in Montana on the ranch that your granddaddy homesteaded, and it's not because your mean big brother used to beat you up.

You stand strong in *your* spirit because you are filled with *God's* Spirit. But you are only strong in your spirit because you are, in and of yourself, weak. Paul said, "When I am weak, then am I strong" (2 Cor. 12:10). You have such limited power of your own that you need to keep asking for God's Spirit to fill you up. And that keeps you growing stronger all the time.

To stand strong in God's Spirit is the only way to truly stand strong. All the other kinds of strong standing are like mere shadows of the real thing. It is a level of stamina that believes God regardless. It is simply knowing who God is, knowing that you can trust Him to be who He says He is, trusting Him to do what He says He will do. Your flesh, persistence, or composure doesn't amount to much compared to His way of standing.

When you stand strong in God's Spirit, you:

+ Walk by faith, not by sight

+ Walk in boldness and authority

+ Speak the Word of God, and situations change

+ Lay hands on the sick and they recover

+ Press forward to do His works no matter what opposition comes your way

+ Are strong in adversity

+ Are calm in the storm

+ Call forth those things that are not as though they were

You can't become strong in your spirit overnight, and it doesn't happen automatically. It's a lifelong process of growth, and you have to cooperate with it. When the disciples wanted to see an example of the kingdom of God, Jesus showed them a child. To become strong in spirit, you must become childlike in your faith.

Sometimes the only way to become strong in spirit is through trials. The early church suffered many trials and tribulations. Paul and Barnabas encouraged them to "continue in the faith in spite of all the persecution, reminding them that they must enter into the Kingdom of God through many tribulations" (Acts 14:22, TLB).

We grow strongest if we grow where we are planted. We put our roots down in Jesus, and we just grow. Storms come through. Droughts come. Hot and cold weather come. We start out like little saplings, but we just keep on drawing the nourishment out of the soil and the air. We grow taller, our bark gets thicker, and we grow more leaves. Eventually, we start to bear fruit.

> The [uncompromisingly] righteous shall flourish like the palm tree [be long-lived, stately, upright, useful, and fruitful]; they shall grow like a cedar in Lebanon [majestic, stable, durable, and incorruptible]. Planted in the house of the Lord, they shall flourish in the courts of our God. [Growing in grace] they shall still bring forth fruit in old age; they shall be full of sap [of spiritual vitality] and [rich in...trust, love, and contentment].
>
> —Psalm 92:12–14, AMP

Jesus, Standing Strongest of All

I love the way Bob Sorge describes Jesus's standing firm in the face of the devil's temptations in the wilderness:

> There is no greater example of an overcomer than that of our Master Himself. When accosted by the adversary [in the wilderness, see Matt. 4:1–11], Jesus had to fight to maintain His stand.
>
> The devil launched his attack by saying, "If You will just bend over and pick up a stone and turn it to bread..."
>
> Jesus said, "I'm not bending over. I'm going to stand right here."

So the devil said, "If You will just throw Yourself down from the pinnacle of the temple in a sensational way..."

Jesus said, "I'm not throwing Myself down; I'm just going to stand here."

So the devil said, "Well, if You will bow down and worship me, then I'll give You everything..."

"You don't get it," I can hear Jesus responding. "I'm not going to bend down, I'm not going to throw Myself down, and I'm not going to bow down. I'm going to stand—and having done all, to stand!"[1]

For Jesus, that was just the beginning. In spite of everything, He stood firm through the years of His ministry (even standing once on open water!), and He ended up standing before Pilate, bloodied and beaten. He was nailed to the cross—in a standing position; think about that—and He died there. Three days went by in which time itself seemed to stand still, at least for His disciples. Then, to their everlasting amazement and ours, they saw with their own eyes that *He was still standing!* Having done all, He stood back up and walked out of His graveclothes. He rose up from the grave, and He went to stand for all eternity in fullest authority, sharing His authority with those who would believe in Him.

A DIFFERENT SPIRIT

It's obvious that someone who stands strong like Jesus has a different kind of a spirit inside. That kind of person does not go along with the crowd. That kind of person does not yield to fear. That kind of person does not compromise his or her faith, even when everybody else decides to do so.

The Bible declares that Joshua and Caleb had a "different spirit" from the rest of the leaders (Num. 14:24, NKJV). They were two members of the select group of twelve that got to sneak into the Promised Land to spy it out for Moses and the people of Israel. When they got back with their report, they were outvoted by the others. It was a majority of ten to a minority of two, Joshua and Caleb.

The other ten spies said, "This is impossible. All of the armies of Israel's tribes will not be strong enough to prevail against those fearsome giants that we saw. The land of milk and honey is occupied already—by giants. Just forget about it. We're stuck here in the wilderness now. "

Joshua and Caleb begged to differ.

> Caleb stilled the people before Moses, and said, Let us go up at once, and possess it; for we are well able to overcome it.
>
> —NUMBERS 13:30

> Joshua son of Nun and Caleb son of Jephunneh, who were among those who had spied out the land, tore their clothes and said to all the congregation of the Israelites, "The land that we went through as spies is an exceedingly good land. If the Lord is pleased with us, he will bring us into this land and give it to us, a land that flows with milk and honey. Only, do not rebel against the Lord; and do not fear the people of the land, for they are no more than bread for us; their protection is removed from them, and the Lord is with us; do not fear them." But the whole congregation threatened to stone them.
>
> —NUMBERS 14:6–10, NRSV

If that had happened to you, what would you do? Run for your life? Go find an empty tent and sulk? Give it up and try to make the best of the situation? Joshua and Caleb didn't do anything like that.

They simply stood firm, even though the other ten spies—and all the people of Israel—disagreed with their wisdom and refused to take the land. This refusal on the part of the people created a crisis of the highest magnitude. God threatened to cancel His promise and start over with new people. (See Numbers 14:11–12.) But Moses persuaded the Lord to stay His hand—for a high cost. Now they would have to endure a forty-year wilderness trek and the slow attrition of all of the unwilling masses.

Joshua and Caleb, to their everlasting credit, didn't add insult to injury and rebel against Moses's leadership, even if they may have privately disagreed with it. They just stuck to their original evaluation—"Yes, we can conquer that land. It's ours. God has given it to us."—without wavering, for forty long, dusty years in the wilderness.

In the long run, after persevering, they won. Even Moses didn't get to possess the land. But Joshua and Caleb did, and they remained as strong in both body and spirit as they had been when they were fresh from their spying mission forty years before: "'Now behold,' [Caleb said] 'I am eighty-five years old today. I am still as strong today as I was in the day Moses sent me; as my strength was then, so my strength is now, for war and for going out and coming in'" (Josh. 14:10–11, NAS).

How about you? Has God spoken a word to you or your family that has not yet come to fruition? Have you stood strong against the temptation to give up the fight? Everything that God has said shall and will come to pass. Do not grow weary. Ask God to give you a different spirit, as He did for Joshua and Caleb. He will do it. When the enemy comes at you like a flood, the Lord will raise up a standard on your behalf. And if God be for us, who can be against us? You can stand strong.

We're in Perilous Times

Pastor Jack Hayford, who is the founding pastor of The Church On The Way in Van Nuys, California, says that he sought God about all the disasters of 2005 (the tsunami and hurricanes Wilma, Rita, and Katrina). At the end of his fasting and praying, the Lord said only one thing: "These are [only] the beginning of sorrows" (Matt. 24:8).

The apostle Paul, toward the end of his life, warned of "perilous times" that would be coming in the future. "This know also, that in the last days perilous times shall come" (2 Tim. 3:1). Now we are living in the midst of them. The whole world is in trouble. People's personal lives, as well as whole nations, are falling apart. People are looking everywhere for direction.

In the midst of these perilous times, people are looking for examples. They are looking for rays of light that will help them see where to go. They are looking for help to get through the situations they're in. The floodwater is coming up, and people know they can't swim. The water is rising, and they don't know what to do.

It's not going to be a new president of the United States (or an old one) who will solve it. It's not going to be more Republicans than before or more Democrats than before. It's going to be God who will save us, and it has to be God's people, standing strong and steady, who will show other people the way.

Jesus declared in Luke 18:8 (TLB), "When I, the Messiah, return, how many will I find who have faith [and are praying]?" He is asking if, at the end of this age as we know it, with all of hell's forces coming against us at every turn, He will find people who seek Him passionately and consistently, expecting Him to answer. Yes or no?

When the water is coming up and people are going to die, they're looking for someone who says, "Over here! Watch me. Follow me. I'll show you the way out of there." People are looking for somebody who even *looks* as if they know where they're going, people who are strong and stable in their faith and in the Word. They won't be fussy about who's throwing them a life preserver. A drowning person is not going to say, "No, thanks. I won't catch it, because you're a left-handed Hispanic." No, if they're drowning, as the world is drowning in fear, sickness, and poverty, they don't care who throws them the life preserver. They just want to be saved. They want to find security to replace their desperate uncertainty.

They can find security where you are standing, on the Rock that is Jesus Christ. His strength is your strength. His authority is yours, and so is His power. The same power that raised Jesus from the dead is in *you* to lay hands on the sick, to cast out devils, to prophesy, and to go forth and declare the Word with boldness, clarity, and anointing.

People are waiting for you to help them find secure footing on the Rock. Somebody has to lead them to the One who is higher than we are. It gets personal. God uses you to show people how to get out of the same situations you have been in. You reach out and say, "I know what it feels like to be depressed. I know what it feels like to have your shutters down. I know what it feels like not to be able to cook, not to be able to take a bath for a week. I've been there, too. I've been through depression. But God brought me through, and if you come and follow me, I'll lead you out." You say, "I've been divorced, too. I know how horrible it is. I know how hard your life is. I know what it's like to be with those kids. I know what it's like trying to explain the situation on holidays. I know what divorce feels like. I've been there. Come on, I'll help you through."

Jesus has helped and is helping you get out of your mess so you can reach out and help somebody else. You are able to stand strong now, and it's time to lend some of your strength (which is His strength) to somebody else. The Bible plainly tells us why we go through some things we don't understand: "So when we are weighed down with troubles, it is for your benefit and salvation! For when God comforts us, it is so that we, in turn, can be an encouragement to you" (2 Cor. 1:6, NLT).

After Paul warned Timothy, in detail, about what "perilous times" would consist of, he went on to give him this simple advice: "But continue thou in the things which thou hast learned and hast been assured of, knowing of whom thou hast learned them" (2 Tim. 3:14). In other words, Timothy, "Stand strong."

Get Caught Up With Christ

We can say, "I may not know everything that you're going through, but I know Jesus. I know He has been this way before. You can hook yourself onto me, and I'll hook onto Jesus for you. And you can hook somebody else onto you. They can hook somebody else onto them, and Jesus will lead us all out of this mess. Through His blood and His cross, we'll reach home safely. Just hook onto me. As I follow Christ, you follow me. I'm hooked onto Him, and *I will not let go.* I'm going to be like Caleb and Joshua."

At the beginning of his life as a Christian, Paul used to refer to the "gospel of God" and the "gospel of Christ." But by the time he wrote his first letter to the church in Thessalonica, he was standing so much closer to Jesus that he referred to the good news as *"our gospel"*:

> We know, brethren beloved by God, that he has chosen you; for *our gospel came to you not only in word, but also in power and in the Holy Spirit and with full conviction.* You know what kind of men we proved to be among you for your sake. And you became imitators of us and of the Lord, for you received the word in much affliction, with joy inspired by the Holy Spirit; so that you became an example to all the believers.
> —1 Thessalonians 1:4–7, rsv, emphasis added

Christ's gospel is our gospel, too. It's the same way with you and me as it was with Paul: the more we get caught up with Him, the stronger we stand in His power and purpose.

Grace in Action

"Standing" sounds like a passive thing to do, but it's not. Standing strong, with your spirit linked to the Holy Spirit, is one of the most *active* things you can do. Standing strong means seeing God's grace in action in your life.

That's how Peter saw it: "I have written to you briefly, exhorting and testifying that this is the true grace of God. Stand firm in it!" (1 Pet. 5:12, NAS). What had he been mentioning in his letter? What was this "true grace of God"? The true grace of God in action is:

- Being born again, or saved (1 Pet. 1:3–4, 9, 23)

- Being sanctified and "sprinkled with the blood of Jesus" (1 Pet. 1:2)

- Enjoying a full measure of Christ's peace (1 Pet. 1:2; 3:8, 14)

- Having the fullest joy (1 Pet. 1:6, 8)

- Having God's protection and knowing it (1 Pet. 1:5)

- Enduring (and passing) the tests and trials sent by God (1 Pet. 1:6–7; 4:19; 5:10)

- Giving up all sinning: envy, hypocrisy, dishonesty, lust, slander, evil intentions (1 Pet. 2:1, 11; 4:1–3)

- Resisting the devil (1 Pet. 5:9)

- Receiving God's mercy (1 Pet. 2:10)

- Growing in holiness (1 Pet. 1:14–15)

- Living in hope (1 Pet. 1:13)

- Overcoming fear and anxiety (1 Pet. 5:7)

- Making up your mind to serve God (1 Pet. 1:13)

- Doing good deeds (1 Pet. 2:12)

- Being hospitable (1 Pet. 4:9)

- Looking after each other (1 Pet. 5:1–5)

- Loving your fellow believers (1 Pet. 1:22; 3:8; 4:8)

- Honoring all men, whether believers or not (1 Pet. 2:17)

- Proclaiming the excellencies of Christ (1 Pet. 2:9, 12)

- Submitting willingly to human authorities, no matter how they act (1 Pet. 2:13–14, 18)

- Bearing up under unjust treatment (1 Pet. 2:19; 3:14, 17)

- Maintaining your marriage well (1 Pet. 3:1–7)

- Staying humble (1 Pet. 3:8; 5:5–6)

- Blessing everyone, even your enemies (1 Pet. 3:9)

- Keeping a good conscience (1 Pet. 3:14)

- Praying ceaselessly (1 Pet. 3:12; 4:7)

- Staying alert and ready for action (1 Pet. 5:8)

No passivity. No more wavering. No uncertainty. What you do after you get saved is to *stand strong*. It's living, day in and day out, by faith in the One who saved you and who now lives in the temple of your heart.

Stand in the Full Armor of God

Jesus, who saved you, makes sure you can stand strong in any situation. When you first declared that Jesus is your Lord, you joined the army of the kingdom of God whether you realized it or not. Now He is the one who arms you and trains you for battle, and He's the one who protects you as you fight.

Flip back to the beginning of this chapter and reread Ephesians 6:13–17, the well-known lines about standing in the full armor of

God. I want to look at what it means to be well armed to withstand the enemy on the battlefield of faith. (You might even want to read this part of the chapter standing up! Go ahead, get on your feet—in front of a mirror—and put on the strong armor of God, piece by piece.)

When you stand in the full armor of God, you are fully equipped and ready for anything. First, you are wearing the "sturdy belt of truth" (also called the "loin belt"), which is the Word, God's truth as it is written in the Bible. The belt of truth is of vital importance, because *the Word of God holds everything together.* Without that belt, it would all fall apart.

When you stand in the full armor of God, you are also wearing "the body armor [breastplate] of God's righteousness," which protects your heart [spirit] and other vital organs. King Solomon, who was a wise and mighty warrior, said, "Keep [guard] thy heart with all diligence" (Prov. 4:23). You have to keep that piece of armor on all the time, even when you're asleep.

When you stand in the full armor of God, you are also wearing "shoes of peace," which, if you're talking about standing strong, are among your most important pieces of battle armor. Did you know that the shoes of a Roman soldier, which Paul would have had in mind as he wrote this part of his letter to the Ephesians, were actually studded with *spikes* on the bottom? Far from being stylish little sandals, the shoes themselves were lethal weapons. When a soldier found himself in hand-to-hand combat with an enemy, he could dig the spikes of his shoes into the dirt and hold his ground—nobody could knock him off his feet. His shoes also had "greaves" attached to them—metal plates that extended all the way up to his knees. This made him able to march through rocky and thorny territory without injury, and it meant that a blow to his shins or calves would just bounce off.[2] Like those Roman soldiers' shoes, the shoes of God's peace hold us immovable when the devil tries to push us down. They enable us to press on in spite of discomforts that would otherwise disable us. Lastly, the shoes of God's peace can serve as weapons in a pinch, because those spikes can be pretty vicious weapons. When the devil goes down in front of you, a few good *stomps* will finish him off!

When you wear the full armor of God, you are holding on to the shield of faith. Many people read that part of the passage wrong. In verse 16 of the King James Version, they see the words, "above all" hold the shield of faith, and they think that means the shield is the most important part of your armor. No, the words "above all" mean you're supposed to hold the shield *above* everything else. That's the *position* that your faith should have over the other pieces of armor. It's better translated, "out in front of them all." And before you can hold something out in front, you need to "take" it: "Take the shield of faith." You can pick it up and put it down. You have to make a conscious decision to pick it up.

Another one: when you stand in the full armor of God, you put on salvation as your helmet. What does that look like? I am convinced that it looks something like a Roman soldier's helmet, which was ornate, decorated with all kinds of engravings. A Roman helmet looked more like a beautiful piece of artwork than a soldier's head covering. But it was so strong and massive that nothing could pierce it, not even a battle-ax, which was used to cut off heads. This helmet was awesomely beautiful, the same way that your saved spirit should be beautiful to other people, and yet it was completely effective as a protection. Your salvation is an intricate, elaborate, ornate, and gorgeous gift from God. And if you "keep it on," it prevents the enemy from "cutting off your head" by filling it with his lies.

He can't get close enough to cut off your head anyway, not if you have the sword of the Spirit of God. When you stand in the full armor of God, you take your sword in your other hand, the sword of the Spirit, which is the *rhema*, or spoken, word of God.

The *rhema* word is the quickened word, or what we sometimes refer to as the "now" word, straight from God for you, for this moment in the battle. A sword is used in close combat. That's how you use a "now" word of God as a weapon. It's as if the Holy Spirit, who sees the enemy breathing murderous threats in your face, immediately puts a spiritual dagger into your hand so you can insert it into the enemy's heart.

In Greek, the word *sword* is *machaira*, and it applied to a short, daggerlike sword that was designed to cut flesh. The tip of it was often turned upward, and sometimes it was even twisted, like a corkscrew. It was deadly. Anybody who got that sword driven into him was dead on the spot. When your enemy sees you coming at him with your *machaira*, he grows cold with fear. He's dead. He's gone. He's defeated now, and he knows it.

The kingdom of darkness does not have anything similar in its arsenal. Your enemy may try to talk you out of using it, but you don't have to listen to him. He'll say, "You're too sick…you're too depressed…you're too weak…," but you'll keep saying, over and over, out loud, "The joy of the Lord is my strength! Get out of my way, devil. Get off this battlefield. The Lord has spoken. I'm coming through, and I'm not stopping!"

Fully armed, fully protected, fully *full* of God. You have everything you need for any battlefield you will ever stand on.

For the Sake of Others

It's not just for our own sakes that we get saved. It's not just for pie-in-the-sky by-and-by. It's for other people's sakes. It's for your sons and daughters. It's for your husband or wife. It's for your relatives. It's for your friends, neighbors, and co-workers—for anybody who crosses your path. You're part of the defending army, and you're armed. Stand strong in your full armor of God, and you'll be ready when people need to hook onto you and Jesus. Stand strong in the grace of Jesus, all of the time.

You can't do it just on Sunday. You can't stand strong only when you're hooked onto someone like your pastor. You have to grow up. You have to learn what it means to stand strong. It will help to hear good preaching about standing strong in Christ. You can benefit from reading a book like this one. But for the most part, you learn what it means to stand strong by just doing it.

In Psalm 27, David said, "I would have lost heart, unless I had believed that I would see the goodness of the LORD in the land of the living. Wait [in faith] on the LORD; be of good courage, and He shall strengthen your heart; wait, I say, on the LORD!" (vv. 13–14, NKJV).

Let's keep looking at what that means.

They that wait upon the LORD shall renew their strength; they shall mount up with wings as eagles; they shall run, and not be weary; and they shall walk, and not faint.

—Isaiah 40:31

Conduct yourselves in a manner worthy of the gospel of Christ; so that whether I [Paul] come and see you or remain absent, I may hear of you that you are standing firm in one spirit, with one mind striving together for the faith of the gospel.

—Philippians 1:27, NAS

CHAPTER 3

HOW TO WALK IN THE SPIRIT

BEFORE our two daughters were born, my husband, Jamie, and I used to go on a short-term mission trip every summer. We would choose a country, raise the money, and take a month out of our schedule. In the early '90s, we went to Tirana, the capital of Albania. We had been invited by the government of Albania. Apparently, they thought it would be intriguing to have us come because I'm a Native American.

When we got there, sure enough, the city was plastered with posters with my picture on them and an invitation that translated something like, "Come hear a girl who sings like Whitney Houston." They got that one real wrong—but it got us into the country.

When he picked us up, our host said, "Do you mind going on national television tomorrow?"

"Not a bit," I replied.

So the next morning, they came to the hotel to take my husband and me to the TV studio. There, a beautiful eighteen-year-old girl who spoke fluent English said, "I want to brief you on what's going to happen. These are some questions I'm going to ask you for the interview. We're going to be talking about the concert..." A concert

33

had been scheduled for a huge, lovely government hall. While we got ourselves settled on the set, we talked about the questions.

Soon the floorman announced, "Thirty seconds to air time," and he began to count down, "29, 28, 27...5, 4, 3, 2, 1." When he got to "1," the *loudest* rock music I ever heard in my entire life came through the monitors. On the back wall was a video screen, and I could see a video of Michael Jackson dancing up a storm and singing.

I just froze. "What's this?"

My interview hostess said, "Didn't they tell you? This is MTV."

So, with Michael Jackson gyrating on the wall behind us, I proceeded to tell the audience how Jesus can change your life, how He's the answer to what you're going through. The unusual circumstances didn't matter because there was an anointing!

As a result of that interview, hundreds of young people came to that concert, and many of them gave their lives to Jesus. And that's not all that happened.

Leaving Albania, people had warned us to expect trouble at the border. We knew this could be true, having had past experiences with difficult border guards. Sure enough, the devil knew we were there on God's business, and the guards started to hassle the people in our team who were ahead of us in line.

When it was my turn, I walked up to the guard. He spat out the word, "PASSPORT!" and held out his square hand. I looked him straight in the eye just as lovingly as I could, and I very gently gave him my passport. He looked at the passport, and he looked at me. Looked again at the passport and looked at me. Suddenly his face split into the biggest grin, and I will never forget it because his front two teeth were missing. Through his grin, he said, "Ah—MTV! Yes! Yes!" and he waved us through.

Do you see what God did? I went to Albania expecting to minister to a small group of people, and I ended up speaking to the whole country. I didn't expect that number of conversions, and I definitely didn't expect my MTV appearance also to be my ticket across the border. This is a dramatic example of the results of simply walking in the Spirit. With the Spirit of Jesus inside you, you can expect the unexpected to happen.

Sitting, Walking, Standing

If you're not walking in the Spirit already, you certainly can't *stand* in the Spirit as the people in the Bible did. In the Christian life, as you do in your everyday life, sometimes you lie down and rest. Sometimes you sit. And, assuming your legs work all right, you get from place to place by walking. And when you get there, you stand.

Years ago a Chinese pastor named Watchman Nee wrote a little book called *Sit, Walk, Stand*. It's still in print and translated into many languages. That book, which was based on the Book of Ephesians, described the connections between three postures. Christians must start by sitting—resting alongside Jesus, the Savior who has done all the work necessary to allow believers to enter into new life. Then we get up and begin to walk in obedience to our Lord, learning along the way all about this new life in God. From time to time, we must take a stand against the enemy and for the things of God.

The whole time we are walking and standing, we remain "seated in the heavenly places" with our Lord. In a discussion of the sixth chapter of Ephesians, Nee wrote:

> We have our position with the Lord in the heavenlies, and we are learning how to walk with Him before the world; but how are we to acquit ourselves in the presence of the adversary— His adversary and ours? God's word is: "Stand!" "Put on the whole armour of God that you may be able to stand against the wiles of the devil." The Greek verb "stand" with its following preposition "against" in verse 11 really means, "hold your ground." It is not a command to invade a foreign territory. Warfare, in modern parlance, would imply a command

to "march. " Armies march into other countries to occupy and to subdue. God has not told us to do this. We are not to march but to stand. The word "stand" implies that the ground disputed by the enemy is really His, and therefore ours. We need not struggle to gain a foothold on it.[1]

Do you see the connection between walking and standing—and sitting? Ever since the day you were born again, you have had the privilege of sharing in Jesus's kingdom authority. Spiritually speaking, you are sitting with Him in the heavenly realm. Here in your earthly life, you have learned to "sit at His feet" as Mary did (Luke 10:39), and then to arise and go about His business, being changed in the process into someone who reflects His character, His authority, and His love. From time to time, you find it necessary to stand strong against the enemy, and you can be as immovable as the Rock because of your secure, high seat next to your Lord. So we see that *sitting, walking,* and *standing* are all facets of living in the Spirit.

For short, we call this the "Christian walk," but it's no little stroll around the neighborhood. Sometimes you sweat. (I certainly do, as anyone can attest who has ever watched me preach!) Sometimes you hurt. You may or may not have company along the way.

But, as the Scriptures declare, it's rich in blessings and full of love, "and peace, and joy in the Holy Ghost" (Rom. 14:17).

BENEFITS OF WALKING IN THE SPIRIT

Do you know what I'm talking about when I declare that there are blessings that are waiting for anybody who gets serious about his or her spiritual walk? I hope you don't have to just take my word for it. I hope you've had a taste already—a *big* taste!

When you're walking in the Spirit, you walk in the *abundant life.* (See John 10:10.) You have *peace* in your heart, even when circumstances around you are falling apart. (See Romans 8:6.) You have sweet *communion*—two-way conversation—with God. (See

2 Corinthians 13:14.) You walk right out of your diseases, including your mental, physical, and spiritual sicknesses, and into *healing*. (See 1 Peter 2:24.)

When you're walking in the Spirit, you'll never again spend your days and nights dreading the next day. You'll never feel like you're missing your full potential. You'll have Somebody to talk to when you have questions or when you run into something that's distressing. You'll have the wisdom to raise your children to be balanced, productive citizens of the kingdom of heaven. You'll be a good wife or husband, and you'll learn how to love your family better than you have ever been loved yourself. You'll even be able to love your enemies, and you'll know how to handle conflicts, because the Holy Spirit will help you.

When you're walking in the Spirit, you'll never get too old to stop growing. You'll find something interesting around every corner. You won't need to immerse yourself in entertainments or distractions, because your everyday life will be fulfilling.

You'll become the person you always wanted to be: secure and confident, resilient and strong, wise and generous, and grateful every morning for new mercies and grace.

When you're walking in the Spirit, you're walking in powerful new life. As Paul wrote to the church in Rome, "Just as Christ was raised from the dead by the glorious power of the Father, now we also may live new lives" (Rom. 6:4, NLT). When you walk (and sit and stand) in the Spirit, you'll enjoy the journey!

The School of Walking

The Bible says that Enoch walked with God: "And Enoch walked with God after he begat Methuselah three hundred years, and begat sons and daughters.... And Enoch walked with God: and he was not; for God took him" (Gen. 5:22, 24). Enoch walked with God for a lot longer than most of us will, and it appears that he did a good job of it, because God spared him from the death process. It was a miracle. He walked with God, and then God just took him up to heaven.

We'd like to know more, but we just don't get a lot of details about Enoch's walk. We see his name listed in the ancestry of Jesus. (See Luke 3:37.) We see his name again in Hebrews 11, the "faith chapter" of the letter to the Hebrews:

> By faith Enoch was taken so that he did not experience death; and "he was not found, because God had taken him." For it was attested before he was taken away that "he had pleased God." And without faith it is impossible to please God.
>
> —HEBREWS 11:5–6, NRSV

From that we learn that he "pleased God" and that his strong faith in God was his best attribute. We also learn that Enoch shared God's perspective about people who spurn God's ways, because we also find his name in Jude's letter, in conjunction with a prophetic word about God's judgment upon ungodly people.[2]

> It was also about these that Enoch, in the seventh generation from Adam, prophesied, saying, "See, the Lord is coming with ten thousands of his holy ones, to execute judgment on all, and to convict everyone of all the deeds of ungodliness that they have committed in such an ungodly way, and of all the harsh things that ungodly sinners have spoken against him."
>
> —JUDE 14–15, NRSV

If we want to learn something from Enoch—and we do, because we're trying to understand how to "walk in the Spirit"—we have to summarize his walk in a few key words. All of the information we can gather about Enoch points to the high importance God places on *walking with Him in righteous faith.*

Good Old Gideon

Let's talk a little more about Gideon. We know more about Gideon than we do about Enoch. In fact, several chapters of the Book of Judges are devoted to stories of his exploits and strong leadership. Like Enoch, he too is listed in the Book of Hebrews. (See Hebrews 11:32.) I mentioned Gideon in chapter 1 as an example of somebody who stood strong in God's strength. His story is told and retold because of the way he fought a victorious battle with only a fraction of his troops. Gideon walked so closely with God that he could move in obedience to what seemed like a ridiculous requirement: "The LORD said unto Gideon, The people that are with thee are too many for me to give the Midianites into their hands, lest Israel vaunt themselves against me, saying, Mine own hand hath saved me" (Judg. 7:2).

So Gideon spoke to the troops, and twenty-two thousand of them went home, leaving ten thousand. But that was still too many. God said:

> The people are yet too many; bring them down unto the water, and I will try them for thee there: and it shall be, that of whom I say unto thee, This shall go with thee, the same shall go with thee; and of whomsoever I say unto thee, This shall not go with thee, the same shall not go. So he brought down the people unto the water: and the LORD said unto Gideon, Every one that lappeth of the water with his tongue, as a dog lappeth, him shalt thou set by himself; likewise every one that boweth down upon his knees to drink. And the number of them that lapped, putting their hand to their mouth, were three hundred men: but all the rest of the people bowed down upon their knees to drink water. And the LORD said unto Gideon, By the three hundred men that lapped will I save you, and deliver the Midianites into thine hand: and let all the other people go every man unto his place.
>
> —Judges 7:4–7

That meager number of men—only three hundred of them—managed to rout the vast horde of Midianites and Amalekites. God gave Gideon encouragement, and He gave him a strategy that worked. It was a battlefield miracle that has gone down in history, and it was all because Gideon walked with God.

Now Gideon did not willingly obey God, at least not at first. That fact should give us some comfort as we try to walk with God today. God was asking him to do the impossible, after all. Gideon did not consider himself a mighty warrior, not in the least. In the story, remember the part about the fleece?

> And Gideon said unto God, If thou wilt save Israel by mine hand, as thou hast said, behold, I will put a fleece of wool in the floor; and if the dew be on the fleece only, and it be dry upon all the earth beside, then shall I know that thou wilt save Israel by mine hand, as thou hast said. And it was so: for he rose up early on the morrow, and thrust the fleece together, and wringed the dew out of the fleece, a bowl full of water. And Gideon said unto God, Let not thine anger be hot against me, and I will speak but this once: let me prove, I pray thee, but this once with the fleece; let it now be dry only upon the fleece, and upon all the ground let there be dew. And God did so that night: for it was dry upon the fleece only, and there was dew on all the ground.
> —Judges 6:36–40

Gideon had to be persuaded; he actually dared God to persuade him. And God didn't punish him for that. He just gave Gideon the signs he needed in order to trust His guidance, led him forward, and got the job done. And Gideon wasn't the same man after this happened. He kept walking with God, he kept obeying, he kept protecting God's people from evil, and he kept winning.

So Gideon walked with God, Enoch walked with God, and so did everyone else in the Bible who wears a "white hat." Everybody's walk looks different. The details of each walk will vary. But there are clear common denominators in anyone's walk with God.

Called and Confident About It

Gideon was *called* to do what he did, and with God's help, he gained the *confidence* he needed for victory. Like Gideon, we have to become confident about our own special callings from God. Chances are real good that you and I will not be called to obliterate the Midianites, but we definitely will have to fight against some kind of enemy.

The only way we're going to win is if we're confident about what God wants us to do and confident about the fact that He will go with us to do it. The Bible says, "For we are his workmanship, created in Christ Jesus unto good works, which God hath before ordained that we should walk in them" (Eph. 2:10). "And so, having obtained help from God, I stand to this day testifying both to small and great" (Acts 26:22, NAS). Remember, with your calling from God comes special equipment—a different spirit. Like Joshua and Caleb, you can step out in confidence.

The trouble is, oftentimes, we chicken out. For instance, maybe in your workplace there is a woman who is going through some hard stuff. God speaks to you and says, "Witness." You know what she's going through, because you work right beside her every day. You know how bad her situation is. And God says, "Speak a word of encouragement to her." Or, "Lay your hand on her and pray."

So you gather up all your courage into a thimble, and you say, "Uh, listen, I…uh…I know you're going through some hard times right now. Why don't you put your name and telephone number down, and I'll give it to our committee at church that prays for people, and they'll pray for you. If there's anything I can do, let me know."

Lame, lame, *lame!*

God has given you a different spirit, and He has called you. He has even given you specific instructions. You can be confident that He will obtain results. What are you afraid of? Walking in the Spirit—in confidence—you might say, "Girl, come on with me to the break room. We're going to pray *right now*! I'll lay hands on you in the name of Jesus, and you'll never be the same again."

You can walk in the fullest measure of confidence. When He speaks to you, you won't say, "Wait, Lord." No, you'll walk in obedience the first time He speaks. You have a calling from God, and you have a future. He will usher you forward into your future, if you will come with Him. He will show you who you are in Christ; He will show you where He wants you to go; He will show you how to get there, step by step. As Rod Parsley says, "He knows your omega before alpha ever begins."[3] God is completely in charge, and that's why you can walk in total confidence.

When you walk in confidence, each of your steps is secure and solid. You don't end up wasting time squabbling with your husband or trying to overrule your pastor. You can afford to be calm about it, because you're so sure.

How do I know this? I know what it is like to walk in confidence because, praise God, I do it myself. Also, I know what it's supposed to be like because I read about it in the Bible. Paul told the Ephesians how to walk confidently in their calling: "I therefore, the prisoner in the Lord, beg you to lead a life worthy of the calling to which you have been called, with all humility and gentleness, with patience, bearing with one another in love, making every effort to maintain the unity of the Spirit in the bond of peace" (Eph. 4:1–3, NRSV).

STRONG IN ADVERSITY

Paul also told the Ephesians how to handle the adversities they would inevitably encounter as they proceeded in their spiritual walk. "Therefore be careful how you walk, not as unwise men, but as wise, making the most of your time, because the days are evil" (Eph. 5:15–16, NAS). He didn't say, "Some days might be evil. " He said *all* of the days are evil, filled with adversity and difficulties, and it's up to us to walk wisely through them.

Don't you wish the days *weren't* evil? Don't you wish you didn't have to contend with disease and accidents, with setbacks, with fearful prospects for the future? Don't you wish discouragement, depression, and disputes would come to a standstill? Don't you wish that we could already have the kingdom of God here on Earth with none of the pain? Well, just get used to the idea that pain is part of the deal, because it is.

It's like exercising: "No pain, no gain." After I had my first baby, I had some extra weight to lose. (So did my husband; he had graciously kept me company when I was eating for two.) So we joined this club and began to work out every week. Soon we got the exercise thing figured out. There were different levels of exercise going on in the gym. Over here, we could see the "high-impact" exercisers. These "high-impact" people are really serious. You can't even talk to them. They won't even look at you. If you ask them what time it is, they won't even pay you any attention because they're so busy exercising and they don't want anyone to break their focus. In the middle, we could see the "medium-impact" exercisers. They are trying to get their heart rate up, break a good sweat. They aren't as serious as the high-impact people. And then over there, we could see the "low-impact" people. That's where we felt the most comfortable. Like me, they come to the gym to work off a little extra weight. They get onto the machine because they don't want to feel guilty when they eat that piece of fried chicken.

Guess who got the most benefit from their gym membership? Guess who had the sorest muscles, too? Change the picture from gym membership to kingdom membership. The world around us is in high-impact sin. It's going to require high-impact Christians to counteract that. High-impact Christians have worked hard to be strong enough to make a difference around them. Low-impact Christianity is not going to cut it.

Even on the level of everyday adversities—getting along with folks around us, keeping ahead of emotional storms—we need to get stronger. Sometimes people will hurt you. They've been hurt by somebody else, and they lash out in some way. Jesus points this out in Matthew 24:10 (AMP): "Many will be offended and repelled and will begin to distrust and desert [Him Whom they ought to trust and obey] and will stumble and fall away and betray one another and pursue one another with hatred."

You want to say, "Poor me. I am in recovery. I've been hurt. I've been stabbed, twisted, bruised, and kicked. I have scars to prove it. Someday I will write a country-western song about it." And along comes Jesus or Paul, telling you it's normal; it's to be expected; it's just part of the Christian life you signed up for.

Latch on to the strong Christians around you. Learn from them how to face adversities. Immerse yourself in reading that is soul strengthening. We need all the help we can get, and it's there for the asking. Oswald Chambers, who was truly an example of someone who faced difficulties with faith, wrote this:

> God does not give us overcoming life—He gives us life as we overcome. The strain of life is what builds our strength. If there is no strain, there will be no strength. Are you asking God to give you life, liberty, and joy? He cannot, unless you are willing to accept the strain. And once you face the strain, you will immediately get the strength.[4]

PUT ON JESUS CHRIST

We are supposed to replace what "comes naturally" with something that comes supernaturally. Walking according to our human flesh comes naturally. Walking in the Spirit of Jesus Christ does not come naturally, because it is supernatural. We have to choose to walk that way. We are supposed to "put on" Jesus Christ in the same way that we put on a fresh outfit: "Put on the Lord Jesus Christ, and make no provision for the flesh, to gratify its desires" (Rom. 13:14, nrsv). The more we do this, the more we begin to reflect the character of Jesus.

Paul told the believers in Galatia, "Walk by the Spirit, and do not gratify the desires of the flesh" (Gal. 5:16, rsv). In the Amplified Bible, his instructions read like this: "Walk and live [habitually] in the [Holy] Spirit [responsive to and controlled and guided by the Spirit]; then you will certainly not gratify the cravings and desires of the flesh (of human nature without God)."

If you try to walk and stand strong in the Spirit without paying attention to godly character, you're destined to fail in a big way. If your anointing is not balanced with godly character, it won't amount to anything. If you spend all of your energy in "kingdom work" activity, to the point that you don't have quiet, personal time alone with the Lord, then you will not be able to reflect His character traits to the world around you, because godly character traits won't have a chance to develop. You will be operating in your own strength, and your own strength will never be sufficient.

What are the holy and righteous character traits of someone who is walking in the Spirit? They include moral and ethical purity, self-control and stability, joy, loving-kindness, patience, trustfulness, and faithfulness. As your Christlikeness develops, you will find that your conscience works better. You will definitely have fewer regrets, and you will second-guess yourself less often. You will think more clearly, and your decisions will be better. You won't be too timid, and you won't be too bold and brash. You will be "just right," while at the same time you're not identical to anybody else in the body of Christ.

More than He wants you to have flashy ministries and powerful works, God wants you to be solid, balanced, focused, and sensitive to His Spirit day in and day out. He wants you to spend time with Him in prayer, and He wants you to read His Word. He wants to give you specific guidance (that you can obey without question) because He wants to express Himself through you. He wants to give you authority, power, and boldness. He wants you to be able to do everything with excellence.

You get there by going there; character development is a process. As you walk with the Lord, you become more and more capable of reflecting Christ's image to others. Paul learned a lot about this. He wrote, "We Christians have no veil over our faces; we can be mirrors that brightly reflect the glory of the Lord. And as the Spirit of the Lord works within us, we become more and more like him" (2 Cor. 3:18, TLB).

Your walk with Christ transforms you into the person you always wanted to be, someone whose God-given individuality is fully integrated with godly qualities of character.

FORCEFUL FAITH

Sponsoring a conference called Press, Push, and Pursue has really brought a blessing to many women's lives in the past few years. We have brought in speakers who possess a single-minded focus on Jesus and what He wants for His people. For short, we refer to Press, Push, and Pursue as "PPP," and PPP has become a kind of shorthand for "extreme faith."

I see that kind of PPP faith everywhere in the Bible. Think of the woman with the issue of blood (described in three of the Gospels—Matthew, Mark, and Luke):

> Then suddenly a woman who had been suffering from hemorrhages for twelve years came up behind him and touched the fringe of his cloak, for she said to herself, "If I only touch his cloak, I will be made well." Jesus turned, and seeing her

he said, "Take heart, daughter; your faith has made you well."
And instantly the woman was made well.

—Matthew 9:20–22, nrsv

Jesus didn't make a house call on that woman. She had to overcome her sense of shame and leave her house to seek Him out. She had to press, push, and pursue Him through a throng of people. And her faith-filled effort was rewarded magnificently.

Blind Bartimaeus was the same way. He didn't wait for Jesus to notice him sitting by the roadside. He *shouted* to get Jesus's attention. People tried to hush him up, but he wouldn't hush. He was *so sure* that Jesus could and would heal his blind eyes. And Jesus did, making a particular note of the fact that it was Bartimaeus's faith that healed him. (See Mark 10:47–52.)

Most likely, you can supply similar modern-day stories of your own. Maybe you're in the middle of one right now. Press in to Jesus. Push aside obstacles that are in the way. Pursue Him until He turns and notices you—and answers your heart's desire.

24/7 Worship

In heaven God is being worshiped continually. Here on Earth we are tuning up for the day when we will be full participants in the heavenly symphony of praise. We are learning to praise God throughout the day and into the night. We are learning to maintain grateful and trustful hearts even when the situation is not encouraging. We are becoming convinced that this is supposed to be a lifestyle.

For King David, it was a lifestyle, and it spilled over into many of the psalms we have collected in our Bible. He wrote some of those songs of praise when everything was bright with fresh victory. But he wrote others in the darkest nights while he was hiding from Saul's men, a hunted man, on the run. He didn't let a mere manhunt (of which he was the object of pursuit) get in the way of his praise of God:

I will bless the Lord at all times: his praise shall continually be in my mouth.

—Psalm 34:1

I will greatly praise the Lord with my mouth; yea, I will praise him among the multitude. For he shall stand at the right hand of the poor, to save him from those that condemn his soul.

—Psalm 109:30–31

The Lord is my strength and my shield; my heart trusted in him, and I am helped: therefore my heart greatly rejoiceth; and with my song will I praise him. The Lord is their strength, and he is the saving strength of his anointed.

—Psalm 28:7–8

Praise and worship are our secret weapons. We can stand strong because of them. We can pray our prayers and do our work with a heart full of praise.

Pockets of thanksgiving and praise are tucked into every book of the Bible. Look at Philippians 4:6 and Colossians 4:2, for example. Read the New Testament with praise in mind. Just look at how much praising and worshiping is going on all the time in the early church.

It's enough to make you want to shout. The name of the Lord is worthy of all praise, all the time. Praise Him right now. Lift up your voice in an outburst of pent-up worship!

Well Able to Conquer the Land

We *have* to walk in the Spirit. We have to walk in synchronization and in harmony with the Spirit of God. If we walk in the natural, the giants will always get bigger, and our walk will always waver and wobble.

Walking in the Spirit, we see with spirit eyes, the same eyes that Joshua and Caleb saw with when they declared, "We are well able to conquer the land." Then we can begin to declare what the Word says about our lives and situations. We know the truth, and it sets us free (John 8:32). Around every corner victory is assured when we're walking in the Spirit.

People ask me, "Judy, how can I become mighty in Spirit, walk in the Spirit, stand strong, and live a victorious Christian life, 24/7? How can I know how to defeat the powers of darkness in my life and in my family? What strategies do I take?"

WINNING STRATEGIES

As we proceed through the rest of this book, we will examine six of the strategies that I have found to be most successful. Christians are overloaded with books, seminars, and sermons about how to have more faith, how to walk in prosperity, how to hear the voice of God, and much more. Even so, the Bible very plainly tells us, "My people are destroyed [or cut off] for lack of knowledge" (Hosea 4:6).

Knowledge is so powerful. When a coach knows the strategy of a team, his team can defeat them; when you know details of a sickness, you can understand how to care for yourself.

How much more important is knowledge about your spiritual position? When your mind is renewed in the Spirit and that information becomes part of you, you *will* be different. You might not even recognize yourself. You will be:

1. Confident in your calling
2. Strong in your adversity
3. Balanced with godly character
4. Violent in your faith
5. Persistent in your prayer
6. Consistent in your praise and worship

Does this sound like you yet? Keep reading to learn how to both walk and stand strong in the Spirit of Christ Jesus.

Such is the confidence that we have through Christ toward God. Not that we are competent of ourselves to claim anything as coming from us; our competence is from God, who has made us competent to be ministers of a new covenant.

—2 CORINTHIANS 3:4–6, RSV

Wherefore I also...cease not to give thanks for you, making mention of you in my prayers; that...the eyes of your understanding [would be] enlightened; that ye may know what is the hope of his calling, and what the riches of the glory of his inheritance in the saints.

—EPHESIANS 1:15–18

CHAPTER 4

CONFIDENT IN YOUR CALLING

I grew up as the youngest child in a family of twelve children—eight girls and four boys. My dad was a man who loved God. He was steady, strong, and hardworking. My mother was a passionate prayer warrior, and she had a powerful healing ministry in our local area. (Back then it wasn't called a "healing ministry." You just knew that if you went to have Sister Jacobs pray for you, you were going to be healed.)

I believe that my grandmother transferred her powerful prayer anointing to my mom. A whole lot of that anointing funneled down on me as a result, and it gave me an early start on fulfilling my calling from God. It also gave me a lot more confidence than the average child (or adult) has. This confidence isn't mere self-confidence, because it has always been based on God's work through me. I can truly say that it has rarely been a temptation for me to think that the wonderful results of my ministry came from my own strength. My mother and sisters helped make sure of that.

Six of us girls had a traveling singing ministry, the Jacobs Sisters, and I was the lead singer. My older sisters would encourage me, "Judy, you can do all things through Christ who gives you the strength." "Judy, it is God who has anointed you, and don't you ever think that it is all about you." They never, ever, let me forget that it was *God* who was manifesting His glory through me. As a result, lives were changed, and people were visually moved by the anointing on our lives. I developed a vivacious, energetic, more-than-a-conqueror spirit. It was bred into me, embedded in me, that I could accomplish, be, and do *anything* that God has called me to do.

This isn't to say that my confidence and anointing have spared me from a lifetime of hard work and personal sacrifice. Far from it. In fact, I think those things are part of my calling, and they make me better able to fulfill God's call on my life. They teach me valuable lessons, and they do keep me humble.

To experience this kind of confident walk, you don't have to be brought up in an exceptional Christian home as I was. Confidence is supposed to be part of your equipment as an ordinary (but extraordinary) Christian. Just look at the early church. Those believers did not have Christian homes to grow up in! Many of them started out uneducated and uninspired. But, with the exception of Timothy (who was working on it), none of them were timid about stepping out in obedience to God. Confidence was one of their primary attributes. Paul wrote to young Timothy:

> [God] has saved us, and called us with a holy calling, not according to our works, but according to His own purpose and grace which was granted us in Christ Jesus from all eternity, but now has been revealed by the appearing of our Savior Christ Jesus, who abolished death, and brought life and immortality to light through the gospel, for which I was appointed a preacher and an apostle and a teacher. For this reason I also suffer these things, but I am not ashamed; for I know whom I have believed and I am convinced that He is able to guard what I have entrusted to Him until that day.
>
> —2 Timothy 1:9–12, NAS

Paul was confident because he knew in whom he had believed, and he knew he had been called to follow Him. Starting from wherever you are, you can grow in your secure confidence in God's calling.

QUALITIES OF CONFIDENCE

Obviously, the kind of confidence I'm talking about is *not* human pride or cockiness or smugness. It is not rude or obnoxious in any way. It isn't particularly *self*-conscious at all. The kind of confidence I'm talking about is based 100 percent on the foundation of Jesus Christ.

Not only are we securely "seated in the heavenlies," as I noted in the previous chapter, but also we are aware of our individual calling from God. This awareness increases as you walk in your calling. Over time, you get better and better equipped to fulfill your calling, and you grow more and more confident about it. You figure out what works and what doesn't work. You encounter roadblocks, and God helps you overcome them. You learn from your mistakes; you are teachable. Paul said:

> We can rejoice too, when we run into problems and trials, for we know that they are good for us—they help us learn to be patient. And patience develops strength of character in us and helps us trust God more each time we use it until finally our hope and faith are strong and steady. Then, when that happens, we are able to hold our heads high no matter what happens and know that all is well.
>
> —ROMANS 5:3–5, TLB

As well as being teachable, you grow in holiness, and your holiness includes a kind of humility that is unmistakable. Odd as it sounds, this humility is one of the surest signs of true confidence. It cannot be faked. Someone who is relying on human strength doesn't have this kind of humility, because it is rooted in trusting

God. You *know* you don't have what it takes. You *know* your calling is too difficult for you to accomplish without God's help. You know you're weak, and yet you don't feel bad about that. Why should you? You belong to a mighty God, and He displays His power to the fullest when you let Him replace your own feeble efforts with His.

When you are truly confident in your calling, your life will display certain fundamental characteristics. Instead of being hard, resistant, and dull, your heart will be awake and alert, willing and obedient, loving and tender. Your mind will be aligned with your heart. You will be able to resist the devil's lies about your worth, since he tries to tear down your confidence. You will be purposeful and faithful, stable and reliable. Your words will show forth wisdom.

You will be single-minded, not double-minded. You will have your face set in one direction, and it will be nearly impossible to deflect you. Nobody will have to force you to go in the right direction, because you won't feel like wandering. You will know you belong to God, and you will know you are following Him—for life. You won't yield to temptations to go back to an old lifestyle or to seek adventures that have nothing to do with your calling.

You may be battered by circumstances, and sometimes you may get discouraged or confused. But whenever you stumble, you will always be able to stand back up again and keep moving forward. You will always come back to the feet of your Savior.

GOD'S CHOICE

To become confident in your calling, you don't have to just luck out somehow. No, if you've read this far in this book, I can guarantee you that you are God's hand-selected choice. He wanted you for a daughter or a son, so He made sure you heard His voice calling your name. He didn't check your résumé and your references first (except to make sure that you were *insufficient* for His purposes). He chose you because He knew you would respond to Him, and He knew He could express Himself through your willing heart.

Paul tells us that God chooses what the world considers weak and even foolish:

> For [simply] consider your own call, brethren; not many [of you were considered to be] wise according to human estimates and standards, not many influential and powerful, not many of high and noble birth. [No] for God selected (deliberately chose) what in the world is foolish to put the wise to shame, and what the world calls weak to put the strong to shame. And God also selected (deliberately chose) what in the world is lowborn and insignificant and branded and treated with contempt, even the things that are nothing, that He might depose and bring to nothing the things that are, so that no mortal man should [have pretense for glorying and] boast in the presence of God.
>
> —1 CORINTHIANS 1:26–29, AMP

Aren't you glad He "deliberately chose" you? Your significance comes from that choice, which has already been made on your behalf and which does not depend on your qualifications. Joyce Meyer puts it something like this: "When God calls us, our first response is to make excuses—'Well, God, you know I am a woman,' or 'I am black,' or 'I am fat,' or 'I am not a beautiful person.' Do we expect God to say back to us, 'Oh, you know what? You're right! I'm sorry; I forgot all about that, so now I've changed My mind.' No, God knows exactly what He's doing when He calls you." Now you need only to learn to walk forward in quiet assurance that He is always in charge and He loves you.

CARE AND FEEDING OF CONFIDENCE

The devil doesn't want us to remember that God Himself has chosen us, and he doesn't want us to be confident in our calling. Sometimes the enemy succeeds in making our confidence take a nosedive.

All the devil has to do is whisper a little lie to our spirits. ("*Psst!* Don't you deserve more credit than you're getting?" Or, "If only they knew what you're *really* like inside.") The enemy will come to you and say, just as he told Eve, "Did God really say that and mean it like that?" He tries to make you doubt your calling. He can read in your eyes either a look of confidence or a look of uncertainty. The devil knows both of those looks, and he adjusts his lies accordingly. You have to resist him, while at the same time letting the Holy Spirit provide your strength.

The devil is a liar. I'm so glad that I found out the devil is a liar. I found out that he *never* tells me the truth, so I don't have to listen to him. Even if what he says sounds plausible (and it does, because he makes note of your real-life circumstances when he plants his lies in your mind), his intent is to tear you down. God doesn't do that. God's Spirit keeps pumping new life through you. The only things that God will ever tear down are the lies that you believe.

The time will come when you can just *tell* when the devil is trying to confuse your thinking. With full confidence, you can say, "Satan, you are a liar. I *can* stand strong, because God is my strength. I can do whatever He wants me to do." Keep standing strong. You will get better and better at discerning the voice of your Lord in the midst of all the noisy voices around you.

I will never forget when God made this clear to me. One morning, I was in the shower. (Don't ask me what it is about showers and bathtubs; some of my greatest words and revelations have come while in the shower or bathtub. Maybe the devil doesn't like water!)

The devil began to feed me all these lies, and of course I was giving him an ear. All of a sudden, God spoke to me and said, "Don't you remember Me telling you that the devil is a liar? Whatever he says is the exact opposite." I remember thinking, "OK, he has just told me that I am not going to make it, so therefore that means I *am* going to make it. The devil said that I am not anointed and called to do this ministry, so that means the exact opposite—*I am anointed. I am called.*" The devil is a liar, and you can use that fact against him every time.

Feed your spirit. I cannot emphasize enough the vital importance of cultivating a life of prayer. You absolutely must keep in constant, daily communication with your Lord. If you fail to keep in tune with the Spirit of God, your spirit will wither up. You won't be able to discern the difference between your own thoughts, the devil's lies, and God's quiet-but-powerful voice.

As you faithfully keep praying, you will be transformed and cleaned up inside. God will equip you for both defensive and offensive spiritual battles. Without even thinking about it, you will find that your confidence will grow exponentially. Jesus said, "Seek ye first the kingdom of God, and his righteousness; and all these things shall be added unto you" (Matt. 6:33). "All these things" that shall be added include everything you need to fulfill your calling, especially holiness and unshakable confidence in God.

You become like the One you're seeking. As you look to Him for everything, your character will firm up. Old habits and patterns will drop off you like autumn leaves. The supply line of your spirit will be wide open to God, and He will be able to pour Himself into you, growing new and godly habits in place of the old. It's better than turning over a new leaf—it's the rich, abundant, totally new life that Jesus said we could have: "I am come that they might have life, and that they might have it more abundantly" (John 10:10).

This spiritual transformation doesn't happen overnight, but I promise you that it will happen as quickly as you can handle it—if you keep praying and letting God fill your spirit with good things.

Expect hardships. Don't let adverse circumstances shake your faith or undermine your confidence in God. Adversities are simply part of the deal. If you expect them, you will be more willing to endure them for the sake of your call.

People think that my singing and preaching ministry is glamorous. There I am, up on the stage, all dressed up with great lighting, microphones, and applause. But you need to know that it's not all that easy. After a long day, my feet hurt. My eyes sting. My energy is completely shot after a big engagement, and often I'm expected at the next one before I've recovered from the one before. People don't see our all-night drives. They don't know about my swollen, bleeding tonsils. They don't see me leaving the comforts of home. They weren't there when I said good-bye to my crying girls.

It is all about choices. It's a choice to say to the forces of darkness, "I am the called, the chosen, the anointed, the appointed, and I am bold to heaven, to earth, and everything under the earth, because I know, 'greater is he that is in [me], than he that is in the world' (1 John 4:4)."

Waiting, in Confidence

God chose us before we were born, and He has waited a long time for this day. How much more can we be patient as we work out our call? Because of God's dramatic call to him on the Damascus road, Paul was as confident as he could be about what he was supposed to do. But he needed to wait a long time before he could launch out in his calling:

> [God] called me by his grace, to reveal his Son in me, that I might preach him among the heathen; immediately I conferred not with flesh and blood: Neither went I up to

Jerusalem to them which were apostles before me; but I went into Arabia, and returned again unto Damascus. Then after three years I went up to Jerusalem to see Peter, and abode with him fifteen days.

—GALATIANS 1:15–18

Paul didn't plunge right into the thick of things. Instead, he withdrew into the anonymity of Arabia. He withdrew, even though what God had told him on the Damascus road was this:

But rise, and stand upon thy feet: for I have appeared unto thee for this purpose, to make thee a minister and a witness both of these things which thou hast seen, and of those things in the which I will appear unto thee; delivering thee from the people, and from the Gentiles, unto whom now I send thee, to open their eyes, and to turn them from darkness to light, and from the power of Satan unto God, that they may receive forgiveness of sins, and inheritance among them which are sanctified by faith that is in me.

—ACTS 26:16–18

Instead of proceeding to carry out that call in his human strength and understanding, he went away to the deserts of Arabia. He doesn't tell us what he did for three years. All we know is that finally he traveled to Jerusalem, where he stayed for fifteen days with the apostle Peter. Only after that did he begin to travel around preaching and teaching, and he had to wait much longer—fourteen more years—before he could really begin the ministry that we read about in the New Testament, with the blessing of the apostles in Jerusalem.

Then I went into the regions of Syria and Cilicia. And I was still unknown by sight to the churches of Judea which were in Christ; but only, they kept hearing, "He who once persecuted us is now preaching the faith which he once tried to destroy." And they were glorifying God because of me. Then after an

interval of fourteen years I went up again to Jerusalem with
Barnabas, taking Titus along also. And it was because of a
revelation that I went up; and I submitted to them the gospel
which I preach among the Gentiles.
—GALATIANS 1:21–24; 2:1–2, NAS

Paul was so sure of his calling that he could afford to *wait*. He
"learned the ropes" during those seventeen years. He matured in his
faith. He suffered setbacks, and he didn't always understand God's
reasons for what happened to him. But he kept pressing forward to
fulfill the call of God.

When you are confident in your calling, there is nothing that
can deter you, discourage you away from it, shake it, or stop it. You
don't have to get anyone's permission or go to your denominational
headquarters. You don't have to go to your family and get their
approval. When you are called, you know it by the witness of the
Holy Spirit inside of you. What stands out to me in this passage is
Paul's strong assurance. He had the confidence to pursue his call,
all in good time.

In essence, he said, "I didn't talk it over with anyone; I didn't go
straight up to the Jerusalem headquarters to consult with someone
who had been in the ministry before I was to get their approval.
No," he said, "I went away to the desert, by myself, and began to
seek the face of God. It wasn't until three years later that I finally
went to Jerusalem and met with Peter and told him about it."

Paul was "big stuff" when he was persecuting Christians. Then
he got knocked off his horse, and he gave himself to God's call.
He started over, and he started small. He didn't start at the top.
A calling from God never starts at the top. You'll be working up
toward the top for a long time, and the "top" means something different in every person's life.

CONFIDENCE GROWS BY DEGREES

I started out as a twelve-year-old, tagging along with my family. For years and years, my sisters and I spent our time singing in small churches. We ministered to people one by one in cancer hospitals. We would walk from one hospital bed to another, and we would sing. We sang in jails and prisons. It was a proving ground, a time of testing. Quite honestly, these were the only places we had to sing, and we loved every minute of it. We would fast and pray over every place God would open up for us, no matter how big or how small. In essence, God was seeing if I would be faithful in the small things.

In those years, as time progressed, I began to wonder, "What is God calling me to do next? Can I be trusted to take the next step? Can I learn to keep my eyes fixed on Him?"

During a waiting time, you are getting prepared. In addition to everything else, you are learning how to stir up your gift or gifts. (See 2 Timothy 1:6.) It's your responsibility to discover (with God's help) what He has gifted you to do and, still with God's help, to develop that gift by starting to use it. Your gift will help guide you into your destiny.

If you're relatively young, that sounds like a reasonable thing to do, just as going to school gives you the added training and experience you need to step into an adult role of responsible service. But what if you're already in your fifties or even past retirement age? What's the point of talking about getting a vision from God and preparing for its future fulfillment? You may be thinking, "I just don't have what it takes. I missed the boat. Life just passed me by, and now I'm babysitting for my grandchildren. I don't have enough years left, and I don't have the energy to stir up some gift."

Well, I have news for you. God seems to show a remarkable preference for people in your age bracket. In the Bible, we read about some older people that were sent on some wild missions. They had labored all their lives doing something else, and suddenly they got a vision from God and energy to go with it. Think of Jacob, starting all over in a new country at the age of 130 (Gen. 47:9). Think of Abraham and Sarah. How would you like to be told by God to start a family at the age of 100? (See Genesis 18:11–15; 21:1–8.) Think of Moses. Think of Aaron, too—he wasn't a spring chicken when God told them to tell Pharaoh, "Let My people go." Don't forget Elizabeth and Zacharias (Luke 1), middle-aged and having their first baby!

Corrie ten Boom comes to mind in this regard. She was already a very powerful evangelist and teacher. Yet on her eightieth birthday, she asked Loren Cunningham and his wife, Darlene, to come and pray for her. She said, "I believe God wants to give me a new ministry for my birthday." This woman, who had been imprisoned in a Nazi concentration camp along with her father and sister, and who had prayed and preached for Jesus since then, now felt the call to a new ministry in her late life. So she purchased a red suitcase and began traveling literally all over the world. She touched millions with her best seller, *The Hiding Place*, which Billy Graham made into a life-changing film that was viewed by over nine million people. It is never too late!

HAVING THE VISION OF GOD

In order to respond to your call, you must first grasp the vision of God for your life.

Of course, if you don't want any challenges, maybe you'd better not. Plenty of people settle for cookie-cutter lives, raising their families, going to church, even doing what they consider to be "God's work"—but without a vision or a call. Oswald Chambers was no stranger to this pattern. He wrote:

> It is easier to serve or work for God without a vision and without a call, because then you are not bothered by what He requires. Common sense, covered with a layer of Christian

emotion, becomes your guide. You may be more prosperous and successful from the world's perspective, and will have more leisure time, if you never acknowledge the call of God. But once you receive a commission from Jesus Christ, the memory of what God asks of you will always be there to prod you on to do His will.[1]

God will give you a vision and a call if you ask Him to show you what He wants you to do in your life. It may take a while to flesh out the details, and waiting for your vision to be fulfilled takes patience, but patience is not the same as indifference. In fact, patience conveys the idea of someone who is tremendously strong and able to withstand all assaults. Think of a determined little brother trying to beat up his big brother. His big brother just stands there, solid and firm. The big brother is not going anywhere. He's not moving. Little brother keeps smacking him with blows, but it doesn't bother him. Big brother may even smile. He has the patience to wait it out, and he knows he won't get hurt. In fact, patience conveys the idea of someone who is steadfast despite opposition or difficulty. Think of kids playing a game of tug-of-war. You always put the strongest kid toward the front so that he can dig his heels in and just hold the line. If he's patient, just standing there, the rest of his team can pull the other team across the line.

After talking about writing down the vision of God, Habakkuk prophesied, "The vision is yet for an appointed time, but at the end it shall speak, and not lie: though it tarry, wait for it; because it will surely come, it will not tarry" (Hab. 2:3).

Standing strong while waiting. If you have the vision of God, you have tapped into the source of patience for waiting. You are not so much devoted to a cause or to any particular issue. You are devoted to God Himself. And God furnishes the inspiration both to wait and to fulfill the vision He has given you. In the process of waiting, He teaches you what you need to know in order to complete the picture. James wrote, "Let patience have her perfect work, that ye may be perfect and entire, wanting nothing" (James 1:4).

Moses endured patiently—for more years than most of us have been alive—not because of his devotion to his principles of what was right, nor because of his sense of duty toward God, but because he had a vision of God. He endured as seeing Him who is invisible:

> By faith Moses, when he was grown up, refused to be called the son of Pharaoh's daughter, choosing rather to share ill-treatment with the people of God than to enjoy the fleeting pleasures of sin. He considered abuse suffered for the Christ greater wealth than the treasures of Egypt, for he looked to the reward. By faith he left Egypt, not being afraid of the anger of the king; for he endured as seeing him who is invisible.
>
> —Hebrews 11:24–27, rsv

Moses was looking toward the future, even though he couldn't see it clearly. He was looking toward God, even though God was invisible to his eyes. Moses's patient endurance was inspired by his strong faith.

You always know when a vision is from God because of the inspiration that comes with it. Things come to you with a kind of greatness that they wouldn't have otherwise. There is a certain vitality in your life. Everything is energized by God. You will keep reaching out for more than you have already grasped. You will not be satisfied spiritually, and that's a good thing.

Paul pressed toward the goal, declaring:

> Not that I have already obtained this or have already reached the goal; but I press on to make it my own, because Christ Jesus has made me his own. Beloved, I do not consider that I have made it my own; but this one thing I do: forgetting what lies behind and

straining forward to what lies ahead, I press on toward the goal
for the prize of the heavenly call of God in Christ Jesus.
—PHILIPPIANS 3:12–14, NRSV

Nothing deterred Moses or Paul. Nothing needs to deter you
and me, either. Even if we have to endure a time of seeming separa-
tion from God, when He doesn't speak to us and when we are starving for His presence, the power to endure will be there—because
we have a vision of God. God's own Son had to endure a time of
temptation in the wilderness, but He was able to endure because He
knew there was something to endure for. His Father sustained Him,
and He will sustain us when we keep our eyes on Him, waiting with
patience and confidence.

I like the definition of *vision* that Myles Munroe quotes in his
book *The Principles and Power of Vision*. He says that vision is "fore-
sight with insight based on hindsight."[2]

WHAT IS YOUR CALLING?

Isn't it wonderful for me to tell you about my own experience, or
Paul's? But you may be saying to yourself, "Aren't those examples a
little more dramatic than my experience? How do I know what God
is calling me to do? What does it mean to have a call from God, and
how can I be sure of my own calling?"

Oswald Chambers says that your personal calling can never be
understood completely. Still less can it be explained completely to
other people. Your calling from God is something that you perceive
because part of your internal makeup recognizes the part of God
that it came from. He says it's like the "call of the sea."[3] In other
words, just as a sailor feels beckoned by the ocean, so you might be
called to become a pastor, a counselor, a social worker, or an artist.
You discover the part of God's nature that is in you, and it compels
you to do something.

Compels is not too strong a word. Paul described his call to preach the gospel of Jesus Christ this way: "If I proclaim the Message, it's not to get something out of it for myself. I'm *compelled* to do it, and doomed if I don't!" (1 Cor. 9:16, THE MESSAGE, emphasis added).

If you obey from the first realization of your call, your obedience will put sureness in your step, a confidence that you are doing what you were created to do. Whatever your call is, you can do it with authority and do it with an anointing. You can minister to the body of Christ and to the world.

STEPPING INTO YOUR CALLING

Over the centuries, Christians have assembled a body of wisdom regarding how to hear God's call. What follows here is a list of the main points distilled from that wisdom. I'll discuss each one below.

Above all, you need to learn to recognize God's voice. You need to understand how He speaks to you through His written Word, and you need to know how to distinguish the true from the false in His spoken, prophetic word to you. You need to pay attention to the burden of the compelling vision God will give you, and you need to open your spirit to the vision itself. God will always confirm your calling in some way, and there will always be an open door for you to walk through.

Learn to recognize His voice. There are a lot of voices in the world, and you need to learn what His sounds like. The Holy Spirit speaks with distinction, and He speaks in silences. You need to get quiet in order to hear Him.

The Holy Spirit is your teacher. He's your guide. He's your leader. He's the one who comes alongside to show you where to go. He not only comes alongside, but He is also *in* you. The Holy Spirit resides inside you, and He never leaves you. He gives you plenty of opportunities to get used to what His voice sounds like. His voice is hushed. His voice speaks softly to your heart and says, "Don't go there. Go here. Don't say that. Say this..."

Jesus said that His sheep know His voice, and a stranger they will not follow (John 10:4–5). His voice will lead you and guide you into all truth (John 16:13). When the Holy Spirit speaks to you, He'll tell you to do the kind of things your Father would tell you to do. No other voice is going to tell you to preach the good news or take care of the homeless or move your family to a foreign country.

And the voice of God will give you steps, one at a time, as you obey the instructions you have already been given. The Word says, "If ye be willing and obedient..." (Isa. 1:19). That implies that you are acting on the direction you have. The Father wants you to hear His voice, do what He tells you to do, and do it the first time. And every time you step out in obedience, there's always going to be a greater revelation. You'll hear His voice telling you the next step. You'll get stuck in the process if you don't obey. If you are obedient, you will eventually get the whole picture. "And thine ears shall hear a word behind thee, saying, This is the way, walk ye in it, when ye turn to the right hand, and when ye turn to the left" (Isa. 30:21). All you have to do is take the next step.

So listen to Him. Keep your mouth shut and listen. God speaks in silences. He can't talk while you're busy talking. One time a woman came up to me and said, "Sister Judy, God doesn't talk to me." She wanted me to help her hear God. That woman was talking so fast, she wasn't even breathing! I thought, "I know why God doesn't talk to you." You have to keep quiet and keep listening for His voice. Keep paper and pen by your bedside in case He wakes you up in the night to speak to you. Listen.

The Spirit is the truth. You have a relationship with Him. He will teach you what is right, and He will show you where to go. And it will *fit*. You will recognize it. You'll know what your calling is because it will feel right. You may realize that you didn't do a good job or that you could have done it better, but at the end of the day, you're going to say, "That was 'me.' That felt right. Doing that is what I am." You may have flubbed it up here and there, but you can't ignore the fact that it felt good.

I remember the first time I stood to preach. I'd always told people, "I'm not really a preacher. I just love to testify." Then I received the call of God on my life, and I felt anointed and compelled to preach. I remember preaching my first message. After I was done, I thought to myself, "That was the sorriest message I ever heard. But it sure did feel good. It fit me. It felt good while I was doing it."

Your first attempts may be sorry, too. But acting out your calling feels good to you, inside and outside.

He talks to you through His Word. If you want to get to know Him, get into His Word. If you want to know who God is, what God is, what God says and thinks about you, what God wants you to do, what your calling is, what you are, who you are, and where you are going—get into the Word. Read it. Don't just acquire the latest version of the Bible—*read it.*

Read through the whole Bible. Don't just dip in and out. Get yourself a one-year Bible. Start reading with the date of that day, and keep going. Read it through every year, and read it every day. If you have a call of God on your life, you need to be reading your Bible. It's a no-brainer.

Let the Word of God be your final authority. Never trust anybody above the Word, including yourself.

He speaks to you through prophecy. Prophecy is one of the ways God uses to get you oriented, to adjust your understanding of your call, and to open your eyes to new things that He wants you to do.

I hope you know that you can't automatically trust every prophetic word that comes your way. You need to pay attention to the following precautions:

1. A true prophecy is based on the truth of the Word of God.

2. Your spirit should witness to a true prophecy. Your heart leaps and says, "Yes!"

3. A true prophecy makes sense. Don't believe something that doesn't make a lick of sense.

4. A true prophecy relates to something in your past or present life. If someone tells me I'm going to be a dancer, I know better. I'm just not a dancer.

5. A true prophecy will allow for a time of confirmation. You don't have to feel rushed. God won't say, "You're called to China, and you leave tomorrow. Someone is going to come to your house, pick you up, and put you on the next boat out."

6. A true prophecy will clarify and confirm what you've been feeling all along but haven't known how to express it. If you've been wondering and your call has been kind of cloudy in your spirit and mind, the prophetic word will be "fitly spoken...like apples of gold" (Prov. 25:11).

God will give you a burden for a vision He has placed on your heart. You will be overwhelmed with the thing. It will be on your mind, in your heart. It will compel you. You will want to fast and pray about it. You will not be able to shake it off, even if you try, which probably you won't do.

God will anoint your spirit eyes to see your vision. Close your eyes. What do you see? See with your spirit the vision God has given to you.

God told Joshua, "See, I have given into your hand [the city]" (Josh. 6:2, RSV). He gave him the vision in advance, before Joshua conquered Jericho by using God's strategy. God did not show Joshua the ending, and He won't show you or me the ending either. He never shows us Z first, although He gives us a great desire to get there. He always shows us A first, then B, C, D, and so on. You have to get from B to Y by means of the vision He supplies for you.

God will always confirm your calling. He'll use big things and little things. He'll speak to you through junk mail and radio programs. He'll bring people into your life just so they can say one word or one phrase to you. You'll be reading the Bible, and the Holy Spirit will seem to highlight a particular passage. Your pastor will preach about something that relates to your calling, or your worship leader will sing a new song that speaks to your heart. You get the idea. You've seen it happen.

There will always be an open door. From the isle of Patmos, John wrote these prophetic words: "Behold, I have set before thee an open door, and no man can shut it" (Rev. 3:8). Paul wrote to the Corinthians, "A wide door for effective work has opened to me" (1 Cor. 16:9, NRSV).

It may not be the door you were expecting, but it will be a door, and you can walk through it. It may not be the door you wanted, but it will be the door you need. It may be one door in a series of open doors, because you need to take one step at a time. It's as if you step through a big front door into the lobby, then you go through several smaller doors to get to where you are going.

Your job is to obey each step of the way. Your job is *not to quit.* You can't give up. You have to keep walking. You can't sit down. You have to keep standing strong.

The Father is with you. The Son is with you. The Holy Spirit is with you. The angels are with you. Intercessors are with you. You can't quit. I know I can't quit—even though it seems like I quit about every two days. I just get so tired. I quit for about two hours, and then I just get up and keep going and going. Why? Because I know what God wants me to do. I can't quit. I have no option.

MATURING YOUR VISION

Over time, God may change and mature your vision and your calling. In fact, He almost certainly will do that. When I was a twelve-year-old, going into churches with my family, I never dreamed that one day I would be hosting major conferences, singing and preaching before huge crowds. When I was a young single woman, singing gospel songs in churches, I never dreamed that I would be hosting an international mentoring institute, writing books, or speaking on television and radio. I didn't even know I would be married and have children, and I didn't expect to be helping my husband reach out to married couples in couples' retreats.

It has all come about because it's part of the outworking of the same vision, the same call. It reflects the choices that God has helped me make along the way as I tried to obey His voice.

KNOW WHAT YOUR CALL IS NOT

There are some things you just know you are called to do, and some things you are definitely not called to do, even if your family and friends are called to those things.

Some people, praise God, are called to work intensively with young people. I'm not one of them. I like and love young people, and I end up ministering to them every week, but I'm not called to minister to young people exclusively.

Jamie, my husband, has a calling on his life to minister to married people. I can help him out with that, but it's not my primary calling. I do not have what it takes to sit down with people and work through problems in their marriage. I'm not called to pastor, either. And I don't feel I'm called to move to another country as a missionary. There are a lot of things I'm not called or equipped to do. That's true for everybody.

That's why the Bible describes the body of Christ as having many different parts, just like our physical bodies. The mouth cannot do the same things as the thumb. The lungs function very differently from the stomach.

> For the body is not one member, but many. If the foot shall say, Because I am not the hand, I am not of the body; is it therefore not of the body? And if the ear shall say, Because I am not the eye, I am not of the body; is it therefore not of the body? If the whole body were an eye, where were the hearing?...
>
> Now ye are the body of Christ, and members in particular. And God hath set some in the church, first apostles, secondarily prophets, thirdly teachers, after that miracles, then gifts of healings, helps, governments, diversities of tongues. Are all apostles? are all prophets? are all teachers? are all workers of miracles? Have all the gifts of healing? do all speak with tongues? do all interpret?
>
> —1 CORINTHIANS 12:14–17, 27–30

No, not one of us is called to do everything. We are supposed to specialize, and we need each other. I need you to follow your assignment from God so that I can follow mine. It's pointless and hopeless for me to try to do your job, just as it is for you to try to do mine.

IT TAKES TIME

Earlier in this chapter, I described the waiting that's involved in the fulfillment of the call of God on your life. I want to return to that idea. It takes time to mature in the vision of your calling. You have to work and wait, both.

I use an illustration of a man who loves to eat apples. He decides he wants his own apple tree in his own yard, so he goes to the nursery and buys a little one. He brings it home, digs a hole, plants the root ball of the tree down in that hole, and covers it up with dirt. He waters it and looks after it.

Will the man get apples off his little tree this year or next? No, if he wants apples this year or next year, he'll have to keep buying them at the market. In fact, if he wants to eat apples, he'll be buying them from other people for a long time. His little tree isn't mature enough to produce apples yet. He has to take care of it, and it has to grow bigger. He won't be able to eat his own homegrown apples for years.

It's the same with your calling. You may wonder sometimes if you'll ever see fruit. Your little calling doesn't look like much—yet.

But you *can* stay confident in your calling. It will grow and bear fruit in due season, as long as it originated with God and you don't quit looking to Him. Keep your eyes on your Lord. Stay focused. Don't get tossed around, deflected, or distracted. Stand strong, confident in your calling.

You are a poor specimen if you can't stand the pressure of adversity.

—Proverbs 24:10, TLB

Be joyful in hope, patient in affliction, faithful in prayer.

—Romans 12:12, NIV

CHAPTER 5

STRONG IN ADVERSITY

THE Bible was written about (and by) real people who were also busy people—tax collectors, fishermen, farmers, doctors, and shepherds—educated and uneducated, young and old, married and single. These people went through just about every kind of success and failure you can imagine, and some you can't imagine.

When I read the Bible, I try to read between the lines to determine what people were going through. You can learn a lot that way. Do you know something that you can learn from almost every page? You can learn that you are in good company when you are going through trials and hard times. The people of the Bible were by no means immune to difficulties. In fact, they seemed to *attract* trouble.

Think about Mary, Jesus's mother. Her life was a long series of challenging circumstances. She was a good girl; do you think it was easy for her to be whispered about when she became pregnant before she married Joseph? Do you think it was uncomplicated for her to be nine months pregnant and traveling by donkey to Bethlehem? What went through her mind when she went into labor? Do you think the manger where she laid her baby looked as clean as the one in your church Christmas pageant? Did she appreciate being forced to run to Egypt for safety with her new baby instead of going home to Nazareth? Later, what must Mary and Joseph have felt like when they thought they had lost their twelve-year-old Jesus in Jerusalem? (See Matthew 1:18; 2:13–15; Luke 2:1–7, 41–51.)

After a while, Joseph disappears from the story, so we assume he died. That means Mary had to put up with the life of a single mother, with no pension plan and no health care. Probably her son Jesus, being the eldest, looked after her for a while. But after Jesus had become well established in His father's carpentry business, He left her at home under the care of others, and she could hear only occasional scraps of news about how He was doing, traveling around the countryside as an itinerant preacher. And then—could anything be worse?—she had to watch her firstborn son be tortured and killed like the criminal He was not. (See Matthew 27; Mark 15; Luke 23; John 19.)

It is true that God had warned her early about what would happen: "Yea, a sword shall pierce through thy own soul also" (Luke 2:35). So she didn't expect her life to be easy—far from it. She accepted the adversities of her life as part of the package. Today we call her the most blessed among women (Luke 1:48).

So This Is the Kingdom?

Was Jesus's life any easier than His mother's? He is our best example of how our lives are supposed to look once we're part of the kingdom of God. What did His life consist of? Notice the details. For instance, He was misunderstood most of the time. Nobody except His mother knew quite who He was. And at least once, evidently even His mother and siblings thought He had lost His marbles, and they came to tell Him so. (See Matthew 12:46–47.) Jesus ran into unfriendly crowds (Luke 4:29), and He never seemed to get enough sleep. As an adult, He had "no place to lay his head" (Matt. 8:20,

NIV). He had to watch His step all the time because the religious officials were plotting against Him. Jesus didn't even have any personal support from His closest disciples when He was about to be crucified (Matt. 26:40; Mark 14:37)—after being betrayed by one of His friends.

Not once did He complain that His life was too hard. He didn't seem surprised by any of it. Jesus told His disciples, "The Son of Man must undergo great suffering, and be rejected by the elders, chief priests, and scribes, and be killed, and on the third day be raised" (Luke 9:22, NRSV).

The early church. After Jesus's resurrection, the believers gathered together into groupings of ordinary believers like you and me. We're fond of comparing our modern church to the early church, but we can become too idealistic about what the early church was like. The early church had plenty of whining, squabbling, and power struggles.

Early on, the non-Jewish members of the church in Jerusalem started complaining that they were being shortchanged (Acts 6:1). Two Philippian women, Euodia and Syntyche, disagreed so much that Paul had to ask them in a public letter to stop fighting (Phil. 4:2). In many (if not most) locales, the believers were forced to meet in secret, lest their fellowship be discovered and destroyed. After A.D. 42, many believers, including most of the apostles, were driven out of Jerusalem and forced to reestablish themselves in faraway communities, which meant being separated from family members and sources of income. They had to find new housing, learn a new language, locate some kind of employment, and establish new places to worship.

Everywhere churches were set up, the people had to work their way through an assortment of difficulties. Some of their troubles arose from external persecution, but you know as well as I do that most of it came from internal human issues. Proof of that is the content of the letters of the New Testament, most of which is much-needed teaching and correction. Healthy churches didn't just happen, and both the leadership and the people had to pay a price.

Paul's troubles. Paul's letters give us a window through which we can view the trials and tribulations that he himself went through. There he was, devotedly serving the cause of Christ. Wouldn't you think that he would have had more than an average degree of protection from harm? Wouldn't you think his hard work should have earned him a comfortable retirement, or at least a little vacation sometimes? The Bible does not support that idea.

Apparently, for all the years of his life as a Christian, Paul was continually suffering from the dangers of traveling; he was often nearly overcome by fatigue, hunger, or plain old discouragement. (See 2 Corinthians 1:8.) He sometimes ran into angry mobs who turned on him and stoned him, and he was actually left for dead on one occasion, until the believers gathered around him and prayed for him, and he got up and went back into the city to preach some more (Acts 14:19–20). He did quite a bit of prison time. He certainly didn't get to have a "normal" life. And yet he said, "Brethren, join in following my example, and observe those who walk according to the pattern you have in us" (Phil. 3:17, NAS). And he's the one who also wrote, "I am filled with comfort. I am overflowing with joy in all our affliction" (2 Cor. 7:4, NAS). He even said to King Agrippa, "I would to God, that whether in a short or long time, not only you, but also all who hear me this day, might become such as I am, except for these chains" (Acts 26:29, NAS).

Like Paul, we're supposed to accept trials and adversities as part of the package. We're even supposed to rejoice in them, so that in the end, we can say with Paul, "I have fought a good fight, I have finished my course, I have kept the faith" (2 Tim. 4:7).

The whole Bible is filled with true stories like these. There are everywhere you look. Before He died, Jesus told Simon Peter that he was about to be tested severely: "Simon, Simon, behold, Satan has demanded permission to sift you like wheat; but I have prayed for you, that your faith may not fail; and you, when once you have turned again, strengthen your brothers" (Luke 22:31–32, NAS). As prophesied, it happened.

Have you ever thought about the part that adversity plays in the life of a strong believer? It begins to look as though the *glory* road is kind of a *gory* road sometimes.

The fact of the matter is this—God calls people who can take it. If you can take it, you can make it. You have to be able to take the pressure, the disappointments, the trials, and the troubles. You have to be able to say, "I know whom I have believed, and am persuaded that he is able to keep [me]" (2 Tim. 1:12).

Expect Opposition to Your Mission

I have said this many times, and I will continue to say it: you must know there will always be an opposition to your mission. Whenever you step out and begin to walk in obedience to God, there is going to be some kind of opposition from the devil. As soon as Jesus was baptized by John, He had to face the temptation in the wilderness. (See Matthew 4:1; Mark 1:12; Luke 4:1.)

Your opposition and adversity will take different forms at different times. Today, you may be facing a health problem. Last year, you may have been in a financial bind. Two years ago, perhaps you lost your job. Later on, you might have a lot of trouble with your teenager or conflict in your marriage or a difficult relationship with someone on the job. Sometimes your opposition is discouragement, sleepless nights, or the stress of having too much to do.

God never promised that you were going to float along on this journey of life, smelling roses and never having another problem from the day you were saved. He did promise, "When thou passest through the waters, I will be with thee; and through the rivers, they shall not overflow thee" (Isa. 43:2).

Get it through your head that trials, tests, and all kinds of difficulties are inevitable. God will allow as many of them as you can handle, and He always knows how much you can handle. Your part is to decide now that you are going all the way with Him, regardless of how much it hurts. Usually, by the time you realize what's happening, it's too late to turn back anyway. You can be sure that He will train you and strengthen you every step of the way, because He wants you to be able to take every step in 100 percent faith.

Always remember that the devil brings temptations, but God brings tests. It's all for your benefit. It's all for your growth. The devil brings temptations to drive you away from God, but your God will help you resist them, and He will manage to convert those temptations into soul-strengtheners. They become opportunities for your growth. God brings you into tests and trials, and they may seem counterproductive at first. But He's doing it because He loves you, so you can be pruned and shaped as you grow closer to Him.

Paul said it like this:

> We had the sentence of death in ourselves, that we should not trust in ourselves, but in God which raiseth the dead: Who delivered us from so great a death, and doth deliver: in whom we trust that he will yet deliver us.
> —2 Corinthians 1:9–10

Even if you may feel like you are facing death right now, Paul wanted you to know that *if you just keep standing, He will deliver!*

Giants in the Land

When the twelve spies came back to report to Moses about the Promised Land, the fearful ones reported that there were "giants in the land." That report was enough to deter the people from making the effort to take the land that had been promised to them by God.

Is your promised land occupied by giants at the moment? Do they have names like these? "Insecurity." "Insignificance." "Unemployment." "Deficiency." "Sickness." Who could possibly conquer territory that's being held by giants? Are you tempted, like the Israelites, to hold back and stay safe?

You should know that if you do that, your giants will only get bigger. They're not going anywhere unless God drives them out with His mighty right hand. As a matter of fact, those giants *are* supposed to be there. They are letting you know you are about to come into your greatness and into your promised land—*if* you will stand up and fight.

Some of us started out fighting. But then we started looking at the problems. We started looking at the giants. Stop looking at the giants, and start looking at God. He's bigger.

God wants to show you, by both helping you through hardships and by delivering you from them, how powerful and faithful and loving He is. He is the lily of the valleys (Song of Sol. 2:1). But how will you know that He is the lily if you don't have any valleys? He is the bright and morning star (Rev. 22:16). But how will you even know He is shining so brightly if you have never encountered any darkness? He is the deliverer. But in order to deliver you, God has to have some kind of tribulation to deliver you *from*! He is the healer. But how will you know that He is the healer if you don't ever experience His healing touch?

GOD WORKS IT OUT FOR YOUR GOOD

Opposition and adversity, even the fiercest kinds, are never completely bad. In fact, God always turns around what seems to be meant for evil into something good. (See Romans 8:28.) It's always worth it. You can say that with two black eyes. You can whisper it with bleeding tonsils. You can give thanks from the bottom of a pit. And, like John, even if you have been thrown into hot boiling oil and then left for dead on some remote island,[1] it is there that you will receive your greatest revelation.

What are some of the good things that God will bring out of our difficulties?

Good training. Hard times provide us with *training*. In order to become mature, we need to be trained as children do. We need to get past our tendency to whine and complain about how unfair it all is. We need to get on with the business at hand, learning to respond quickly and obediently to whatever God sends into our lives.

As Joseph Garlington says, sometimes God will say to us, "OK. This is first grade." If we say back to God, "What if I don't like first grade?" He will say, "Then you get to repeat it." I don't know about you, but I want to learn my lessons, learn them well, and move on.

The Israelites may never have learned this lesson, although we can learn from their mistakes: "They turned against Moses, whining, 'Have you brought us out here to die in the desert because there were not enough graves for us in Egypt? Why did you make us leave Egypt?'" (Exod. 14:11, TLB).

Moses responded to them, "'Don't be afraid. Just stand where you are and watch, and you will see the wonderful way the Lord will rescue you today.'... Then the Lord said to Moses, 'Quit praying and get the people moving! Forward, march!'" (Exod. 14:13, 15, TLB).

In other words, the people of Israel had to stop their pointless complaining and obey what God already had told them to do. The Red Sea parted, and they escaped from the Egyptians. When they stopped complaining and followed orders, their dire straits turned into a wonderful deliverance.

In their case, this lesson didn't stick with them. Forty years later, they were still whining. (See Numbers 20.) Sad to say, such lessons don't always stick with us either. But maturity training is still one of the best reasons for having trials. It's as if God has put all of us into His heavenly boot camp. Our latest trials are part of the training process.

Isaiah 30:20 encourages us to believe that "though he give you the bread of adversity and water of affliction, yet he will be with you to teach you—with your own eyes you will see your Teacher" (TLB).

Good opportunities. For Christians, adversities turn into *opportunities.* Hardships give us opportunities to walk in our authority in Christ Jesus (and, putting it the other way around, they give us fresh opportunities to see God's authority at work). When the devil tries to bury you in bad stuff, *that's* when you have the chance to bury him deeper than he could ever bury you. As you lean on God's promises and proclaim His faithfulness, you become an overcomer.

The greatest opportunities for victory arise out of the hardest trials. It's enough to make you want to shout His praises for *not* sparing you! I'm glad He allows me the chance to exercise my authority in Christ. He wants me to participate with Him in ruling in the kingdom. That just can't happen if He just lets me keep "sitting pretty," free from trials and tribulations.

Obvious grace. Unfair circumstances, unfriendly accusations, and ill health provide us with a perfect opportunity to manifest the grace of God. When we are presented with challenging situations, we cannot escape unless we lean hard on His grace. Remember what Paul wrote to the Corinthians? He told them that they had been saved so that the life of Jesus could be manifested in their bodies (2 Cor. 4:10). In other words, while they were still here on this muddled earth in their weak bodies, they were supposed to show forth the glory of God—in the midst of and because of their adversities.

Next time that jealous neighbor of yours becomes a mudslinger, watch God work in you and through you as you don't respond the same way, but rather respond in wisdom and love. The experience may not be much fun, but you can expect God's grace to supply you with the right attitude and the right words. Next time you can't sleep at night, ask for His patience and perspective. Next time you hurt all over and your boss tells you to work late, receive God's help to persevere—with joy.

As Oswald Chambers said, "You did not do anything to achieve your salvation, but you must do something to exhibit it. You must 'work out your own salvation,' which God has worked in you already" (Phil. 2:12).[2] The adversities that God allows in your life allow you to demonstrate His grace.

Good motivation. Without some compelling reason, most of us prefer to sit tight and hope for the best. We don't want to dive into the fray where we might get hurt.

But God loves us too much to let us commit the "sin" of satisfaction. He wants us to be *involved*. To get us off the sidelines, He sends us adversities. It's a rude awakening sometimes.

You might be just bobbing along, floating down the river of your little life, when suddenly you hear a roaring noise. Around the bend, there it is! You are being sucked over a waterfall! You weren't really praying before, but brother, you are now. You were half-asleep just a minute ago, but sister, you are now wide-awake. You are motivated, and you will stay motivated for a while, because you are in the middle of a crisis.

Have you noticed how Romans 10:17 reads? "Faith cometh by hearing, and hearing by the word of God." Not, "Faith comes by what you have *heard*" (past tense). Faith comes by hearing and hearing and hearing. Everybody needs repeated, frequent, even continual prodding and urging to step out on faith. That is why it is so important to keep the Word of God in your heart and mind. Listen to worship music; listen to the Word of God being preached by an anointed man or woman of God. If possible, listen on your stereo, in your car, in your office—anything to keep your faith built up.

"Pray without ceasing" (1 Thess. 5:17). Adversities keep us walking in faith.

In 1993, our ministry operated out of a one-room office in downtown Cleveland, Tennessee. We were paying seventy-five dollars a month for that place, and we had to believe God even for that small amount of rent money. The ceiling leaked. One weekend, we were hit with a monsoon of a rainstorm, and we lost our computer. You have to understand—we had only one computer, and we lost it. After that, we had had enough of this small-faith mentality. We were really determined to pray for the best God had for us. Before very long, God worked a series of miracles, and we found ourselves the owners of the beautiful ministry center on a hillside that we have today. I'm *glad* the roof leaked in that old office! Sometimes you have to step out on nothing and watch God turn it into something. Watch God take what the devil meant for our bad and turn it into our good. Praise God, the devil is a defeated foe!

SET YOUR FACE LIKE FLINT

Once you are motivated to rise to the occasion before you, the next requirement is perseverance. You don't want to wimp out when the ground beneath your feet begins to shake. When you are standing in faith, the wind is going to blow fiercely, and you will want to either sit down or lie down. By God's grace, you need to keep standing. Spread your feet apart and get yourself balanced, good and firm, just in case your storm gets so fierce that you are "tempest-tossed." Sometimes the opposition is so fierce that you are doing well to just hold the line. But that's much better than giving up. You need to keep standing strong. You need to set your face like flint. What does that mean?

When God commissioned the prophet Ezekiel to be a watchman for Israel, He told him, "Behold, I have made thy face strong against their faces, and thy forehead strong against their foreheads. As an adamant harder than flint have I made thy forehead" (Ezek. 3:8–9). Earlier, the prophet Isaiah had proclaimed, "Because the Lord God helps me; I will not be dismayed; therefore, I have set my face like flint to do his will, and I know that I will triumph" (Isa. 50:7, TLB).

When Luke described Jesus's approach to His upcoming death on the cross, he wrote, "And it came about, when the days were approaching for His ascension, that He resolutely set His face to go to Jerusalem" (Luke 9:51, NAS). In other words, Jesus, like Isaiah, "set His face" like flint.

What does this mean? It means that you are absolutely determined to fulfill the Father's will, sure and unflinching in your faith even at the prospect of torture, resolute to the point of continually pressing forward, even if the dangers ahead indicate death. Bible scholar Finis Jennings Dake explains it like this:

> This means to be courageous, firm and resolved to accomplish a certain thing in spite of all the scorn and hatred heaped upon you.[3]

God equipped Ezekiel for the hard work before him. He knew he would have to be bold, hard, stubborn, and unyielding to be able to cope with these hard and stiff-necked people of Israel. Dake states, "God compared the [forehead of the] prophet to adamant harder than flint."[4]

I got to wondering about the word *adamant*, and I did a little study. I found out that adamant is a diamond-hard stone. As a matter of fact, it's the hardest of stone, harder even than flint. When you follow in the footsteps of Jesus and the prophets, you are so determined to fulfill the Father's will that you will not flinch at the prospect of extreme sacrifice and personal pain.

To be that strong in adversity, you must have a calling and a sure word from the Lord that you are in His perfect will. There can be no doubt as to the Lord's word to you. You must be fully persuaded that what God has said, He *will* do. You have to be fully persuaded that His hand is upon you and that you are going to come out on the other side.

As you stand on the Word of God in the face of what seems very doubtful and perhaps unlikely, God will surprise you and go beyond your faith. You can't be shifting back and forth. The Bible says, "Let us hold fast the profession of our faith without wavering (for he is faithful that promised)" (Heb. 10:23).

He will bring you through victoriously. Notice I said *through.* God won't always get you *out* of adversity, but He *will* always bring you *through* it.

Learning to Love Adversity

"Learning to love adversity"? What a paradoxical thing to say! Who in their right mind would want to love adversity? Well, Peter for one. He wrote:

> Beloved, think it not strange concerning the fiery trial which is to try you, as though some strange thing happened unto you: But rejoice, *inasmuch as ye are partakers of Christ's suffer-ings; that, when his glory shall be revealed, ye may be glad* also with exceeding joy. If ye be reproached for the name of Christ, happy are ye; *for the spirit of glory and of God resteth upon you.*
> —1 Peter 4:12–14, emphasis added

In order for the "Spirit of glory" to rest on you, you must suffer adversities.

Paul seems to have been well acquainted with the high personal cost of doing the will of God. You will remember his account from his second letter to the Corinthians:

> I have worked harder, been put in jail more often, been whipped times without number, and faced death again and again. Five different times the Jews gave me thirty-nine lashes.

Three times I was beaten with rods. Once I was stoned. Three times I was shipwrecked. Once I spent a whole night and a day adrift at sea. I have traveled many weary miles. I have faced danger from flooded rivers and from robbers. I have faced danger from my own people, the Jews, as well as from the Gentiles. I have faced danger in the cities, in the deserts, and on the stormy seas. And I have faced danger from men who claim to be Christians but are not. I have lived with weariness and pain and sleepless nights. Often I have been hungry and thirsty and have gone without food. Often I have shivered with cold, without enough clothing to keep me warm.

Then, besides all this, I have the daily burden of how the churches are getting along. Who is weak without my feeling that weakness? Who is led astray, and I do not burn with anger?

—2 CORINTHIANS 11:23–29, NLT

In the Bible, you will find plenty of evidence for the value of adversities. Adversities prove your mettle. What kind of stuff are you really made of? That's always a good question, and God wants to know the answer long before you do. Can you be trusted with His assignments? Will you keep going even when the going gets tough? Will you stand strong?

God will test your character. He will test your integrity. He will test your motivation. He will test your faith. What is the real purpose behind what you are doing? Everything will be tested and tried, and everything that can be shaken will be shaken. You can't go to another level until God proves that He can trust you where you are right now.

God told the prophet Jeremiah:

[But the Lord rebukes Jeremiah's impatience, saying] If you have raced with men on foot and they have tired you out, then how can you compete with horses? And if [you take to flight] in a land of peace where you feel secure, then what will you do [when you tread the tangled maze of jungle haunted by lions] in the swelling and flooding of the Jordan?

—Jeremiah 12:5, amp

Did you see that? God *rebukes Jeremiah's impatience.* In effect, God was saying, "If you can't handle the easy stuff, then how can I trust you with the hard stuff? If you can't even handle it when people talk about you behind your back, how are you going to handle the bigger challenges of ministry, of pursuing the call upon your life, even giving your very life for the cause of Christ?"

Adversities increase your patience. Usually, hard times are not over quickly. Some hardships last your whole life. If nothing else, adversities teach you to be patient. You learn how to ask for His help, persistently, and you learn how to press through in prayer and endurance. You learn how to carry a load for the long haul, and you learn how to *wait.*

Just as David and Abraham and the children of Israel had to wait, we have to wait. Here's what David said about waiting:

Wait on the Lord: be of good courage, and he shall strengthen thine heart: wait, I say, on the Lord.

—Psalm 27:14

I wait expectantly, trusting God to help, for he has promised.

—Psalm 130:5, tlb

Isaiah wrote:

They that wait upon the Lord shall renew their strength; they shall mount up with wings as eagles; they shall run, and not be weary; and they shall walk, and not faint.

—Isaiah 40:31

While you're waiting, you can learn to forget the things that are behind you, the losses that you have suffered, the mistakes you have made. You can put them into God's hands and ask Him to take care of restoring to you what the devil has stolen. Paul said, "This one thing I do, forgetting those things which are behind, and reaching forth unto those things which are before, I press toward the mark for the prize of the high calling of God in Christ Jesus" (Phil. 3:13–14).

What's behind you? You can forget about it, because it's in the past, and the past can't be changed. Forget about the failed marriage, the failures at raising your children, the abortion, the yo-yo weight problem, the adultery, and the financial mistakes.

Get your mouth open, and begin to talk to yourself. Get in front of a mirror. (This always works for me.) Tell yourself:

+ *"I know* I blew it. That thing was meant to take me out, but I won't let it."

+ *"I am* the healed of the Lord."

+ *"I am* going to make it."

+ *"I am* blessed and prosperous."

+ *"I do* have a destiny and a future."

+ *"I am* anointed and appointed."

The devil is your adversary, and he wants to play on your adversity. But the devil is a liar. Don't give him the time of day. Forget about your adversity, and persistently reach upward to God.

Adversities keep you humble. Whether we like it or not, hardships keep us humble. And being humble is requirement #1 for obtaining the grace of God: "Be clothed with humility: for God resisteth the proud, and giveth grace to the humble" (1 Pet. 5:5).

Even a simple thing like getting the "butterflies" before going on stage can be humbling. It is humbling to shake the hand of the hosting pastor with a hand that feels like an icicle. I get nervous every time before I go onstage to sing or preach, and that nervousness keeps me much more reliant on God than I would be if I felt calm. God's grace can ride in on the wings of my butterflies. It doesn't matter how big or small the audience is, I am always humbled that God has chosen to use me. I am always surprised that God is actually using me. I know I am gifted and anointed, but I always get the butterflies, and then I always get to see how well His grace works. I don't ever want to start thinking that I have it all down pat, because it would be then that I would fall on my nose.

Paul suffered from some sort of chronic problem that taught him humility. He called it his "thorn in the flesh." We don't know exactly what his problem was, but he said that it was given to him to keep him from getting proud and self-sufficient:

> So I wouldn't get a big head, I was given the gift of a handicap to keep me in constant touch with my limitations. Satan's angel did his best to get me down; what he in fact did was push me to my knees. No danger then of walking around high and mighty! At first I didn't think of it as a gift, and begged God to remove it. Three times I did that, and then he told me,
>
> My grace is enough; it's all you need.
> My strength comes into its own in your weakness.
>
> Once I heard that, I was glad to let it happen. I quit focusing on the handicap and began appreciating the gift. It was a case of Christ's strength moving in on my weakness. Now I take limitations in stride, and with good cheer, these limitations that cut me down to size—abuse, accidents, opposition, bad

breaks. I just let Christ take over! And so the weaker I get, the stronger I become.

—2 CORINTHIANS 12:7–10, THE MESSAGE

Do you notice that last line? "The weaker I get, the stronger I become." Being hit with hardship is the best way to find out how weak you are and how very strong God can be in you, because then you are forced to rely entirely on God for everything you need.

Adversities show you God's favor. They do *what?* Yes, adversities are undeniable evidence of God's favor. They humble us, chastise us, show us our weakness, prune us of self-sufficiency—and when God sends them, we can be sure that He loves us. Remember the scriptural exhortation:

> "My child, do not regard lightly the discipline of the Lord, or lose heart when you are punished by him; for the Lord disciplines those whom he loves, and chastises every child whom he accepts."
> Endure trials for the sake of discipline.
>
> —HEBREWS 12:5–7, NRSV

I want the Father to always chastise me. I want to be like my little daughter. She wants to learn how to play the piano. My husband and I can see that she has a gift for that, so we're always chiding her about her practice time. If she practices enough, she can be a good pianist. But she won't practice very often unless we urge her to do so. The discipline of daily practice time is hard on her. As much as she wants to grow into a fine piano player, she'd rather be hitting the keys on her computer. How much more does the Father want us to become like Him? "It is God Who is all the while effectually at work in you...both to will and to work for His good pleasure" (Phil. 2:13, AMP).

And when you come out of your trials, you will be pure gold. Job said, "When he hath tried me, I shall come forth as gold" (Job

23:10). Some of us may have settled for just being copper or tin. A few of us have gotten as far as silver. But God wants you to reflect His image. He wants you to be so completely changed into gold that He can start bragging about you, even to the devil.

Adversities enable you to comfort and strengthen others. Another benefit of going through adversities is that they sensitize us to the sufferings of others. After we have learned from our own hardships, we can turn and help other people through theirs, and we can offer them the kind of encouragement that can really do them some good.

Paul puts it plainly:

> What a wonderful God we have—he is the Father of our Lord Jesus Christ, the source of every mercy, and the one who so wonderfully comforts and strengthens us in our hardships and trials. And why does He do this? So that when others are troubled, needing our sympathy and encouragement, we can pass on to them this same help and comfort God has given us.
>
> —2 CORINTHIANS 1:3–4, TLB

After you have grown through a number of testings, you'll have a testimony to share. You will have learned what to do whenever difficult circumstances start to develop. Instead of getting upset and begging God to fix the new problems as soon as possible, you will have learned to trust, stand strong, and pray for more grace to keep trusting and standing as long as it takes. And you will have lived through enough trouble to be able to tell others how faithful God is.

When the people of Israel left Egypt, the desert did not exactly look like a better alternative. But God had a land of milk and honey in mind for them, and that was a lot better than slaving away in Egypt for less than minimum wage with no benefits.

You will remember the time you lost your job, when you thought it was the end of the world as you knew it. And it was—because He wanted to provide you with something better.

Tell others how God worked through your hardships. Show them what happens when somebody stands strong in Him.

Adversities make you more like Jesus. The Lord we follow is "a man of sorrows, and acquainted with grief" (Isa. 53:3). And yet He is the greatest victor of all.

We cannot truly be His followers unless we adopt a "Gethsemane lifestyle," as Rod Parsley calls it. Just before His enemies arrested Him, Jesus wrestled with fearsome invisible enemies in the Garden of Gethsemane.

> God will orchestrate circumstances to cause us to surrender our will to His. Surrender never comes without a struggle. Your soul—your mind, will, and emotions—will struggle with your spirit for control of your thoughts and actions.
>
> Have you bowed your knee in surrender, or are you still struggling?...Living a Gethsemane lifestyle is a continual dying to soul, to self, and to the flesh, and surrendering completely to God's will.[5]

Like Jesus, we also must come to the point of being able to say, "Not my will, but Thine be done. " (See Matthew 26:39; Mark 14:36.)

YOU REALLY DO HAVE HELP

You will feel alone at times and ready to give up, but when you do, remember the story of Elisha and his servant who couldn't see the army of the Lord of Hosts. Elisha could see it, so he wasn't worried about the outcome. All the servant needed was to have his eyes opened to the unseen reality all around him. (See 2 Kings 6:15–17.)

With the help of the Holy Spirit, open your eyes to see the supernatural. In the natural it doesn't look good. But if you can see it in the supernatural, you can bring it forth in the natural. God's strong army is all around you, regardless of what kind of siege you may be undergoing.

Be encouraged, right now. Take your adversities and daunting circumstances, whatever they are, and let them drive you to your knees in prayer. When you stand back up, you will be able to *stay* standing, because God will change your weakness into His strength.

Assign me Godliness and Integrity as my bodyguards.

—Psalm 25:21, TLB

The Kingdom of God is not just talking; it is living by God's power.

—1 Corinthians 4:20, TLB

CHAPTER 6

BALANCED WITH GODLY CHARACTER

OUR ministry keeps us on the road much of the time, and in our travels, my husband and I meet a lot of pastors. One thing we seem to hear from them often—too often—is, "Can you help me find a praise and worship leader?"

One day, a pastor called my husband from California. He said, "I need someone who has an anointing to lead my people in worship, a leader who's in tune with God and who has a spirit of humility. All I want this person to do is to lead the praise and worship. I've got a budget of $100,000 for this man or woman. Can you help me find this person? Is there anybody that you know?" (Jamie told me about this situation, and I said, "Did you tell him *we* could lead praise and worship?")

You see, we have a problem. People who are both gifted and truly faithful are almost as hard to find as dinosaurs. I'm talking about people who are consistent and balanced, people with excellent character, people who can resist the temptations of the flesh. You hear so many stories, and many of them are true. Ministers of music run off with somebody else's wife, or they opt for an alternative lifestyle. Or they simply can't take the daily grind of their calling. And if they aren't treated with star status, then it seems that they are just not "called" anymore to that particular venue or church. They (and often, their volunteer musicians) make commitments and then change their minds as soon as the excitement wears off. They don't like it when God puts them someplace and then the going gets a little rough. They can't stand the pressure, and they don't realize that they have a character problem. They never stay until God is finished refining their characters through their circumstances. They just say, "Well, I don't like this thing anymore. You want me to be here at 6:30 for an 8:00 service? No way. I'm outta here."

I find this trend puzzling, because when I was pursuing the call of God on my life, I did whatever was put before me, whether I got paid or not. To me, it was an incredible opportunity to use my gifts and talents for the Lord. These days what I'm hearing is, "What's in it for me? How much will I be paid, and what benefits will I receive if I choose to play or sing in your church?"

It's not just ministers of music, obviously. It's an epidemic throughout the church. And it's nothing new. King David said, "O Lord, where are the faithful? Where can I just find somebody who's going to do what they promised to do? Where are they? They all talk the talk, but they don't follow through. Where are the faithful ones, those who have grown into maturity of character?" (paraphrased from Psalm 12:1).

David knew what he was looking for. In another psalm, he wrote:

> O Lord, who may abide in Thy tent?
> Who may dwell on Thy holy hill?
> He who walks with integrity, and works righteousness,
> And speaks truth in his heart.
> He does not slander with his tongue,
> Nor does evil to his neighbor,
> Nor takes up a reproach against his friend;

In whose eyes a reprobate is despised,
But who honors those who fear the Lord;
He swears to his own hurt, and does not change;
He does not put out his money at interest,
Nor does he take a bribe against the innocent.
He who does these things will never be shaken.

—Psalm 15:1–5, nas

"He who does these things will never be shaken." In other words, he or she who exemplifies godly character will *stand strong*.

Got Character?

Does true and godly character have to be so rare? God Himself wants to share His character with anyone who will cooperate with Him. In fact, it's so important to God that His people exhibit godly character that He gave us His Holy Spirit to help us. I like this anonymous saying: "Reputation is for today, but character is for eternity."

If you're walking in the Spirit, you are, by definition, growing in godliness. If you're not cooperating with God's refining and perfecting work in your life, you're not walking and growing in maturity in the Spirit. Too many Christians walk around looking as if they've been injected with pickle juice, even when they're talking about how good God is. I believe that when Jesus comes into your life, you should hardly be able to wipe the smile off your face for the rest of your life. You should get a spring in your step that wasn't there before. Everybody will know that you've changed. You have a redeemed character. You're a brand-spanking-new creation.

Godly character includes what we call the "fruit of the Spirit": love, joy, peace, patience, kindness, goodness, faithfulness, gentleness, and self-control (Gal. 5:22–23, nas). You can't argue with the value of qualities like those. Woven into godly character, you will also find more qualities, such as courage, trustfulness, perseverance, loyalty, honesty, reliability, responsibility, integrity, holiness, purity, righteousness, respectfulness, generosity, justice, compassion, mercifulness, self-sacrifice, wisdom, humility, endurance, and more.

Whole books have been written on the subject of godly character, but for purposes of this particular book, I'm giving only one chapter to it. My purpose is very simple: I want to show you that standing strong in God entails standing strong in His character traits.

If you possess a strong, dominant personality, you may think that you already have strong character, but personality and character are *not* one and the same. You can have a strong, dominant personality and be the very embodiment of evil. You can have remarkable charm, powerful leadership gifts, even powerfully miraculous gifts of the Spirit, and have the worst character in the world. (I should also mention that you can also *be* a "character" without having much real character to speak of.)

You *must have* godly, mature character in order to stand firmly on both of your spiritual feet, because your character keeps you balanced through everything that happens to you. With undeveloped or underdeveloped character, you are wide open to danger and failure. The devil is always hanging around, looking for a weak spot, and only your strong character can keep him out.

By definition, godly character involves God. How can you make sure you are growing in godly character? Your character development depends on whether or not you're sold out to God.

BALANCING ANOINTING WITH CHARACTER

When you are old and up in years, how would you like to have fame, reputation, and influence like Billy Graham, Mother Teresa, or Corrie ten Boom? It would be pretty wonderful, wouldn't it? You'd get praise from people while you were still alive and a "well done" from God when you got to heaven.

Well, let me tell you a secret: whether or not you are appointed to a public calling, you *can* achieve the same goal (and enjoy many rewards)—if your anointing is balanced with your godly character, as theirs has been. Anointing absolutely *must* be matched by godly, transformed character. No one has lasting influence in the kingdom of God without maintaining and growing in character, day by day, over a whole lifetime.

I chose those well-known examples because they represent such a good balance between Holy Spirit–inspired calling and Holy Spirit–infused character. What if Billy Graham or Mother Teresa had given up early in the development of their ministries? What if Corrie ten Boom had decided to stay in the safety of her father's little shop in the Netherlands after she was released from the concentration camp? What if any of them had decided that they preferred personal comfort above the clear call of God, a call that would entail countless long days and nights? What if any of them had allowed themselves to fall prey to sin?

Take a brief look at their lives.

Billy Graham

Billy Graham was born in 1918 in North Carolina and was raised in a Christian home. After a very brief stint as a pastor, Billy began to travel. For a few years, until he began to hold evangelistic rallies of his own, he worked first with Youth for Christ and then as the president of Northwestern Schools in Minneapolis, Minnesota.

Eventually, his own evangelistic crusades and related ministries took all of his time. Besides preaching to large crowds, he and his ministry, the Billy Graham Evangelistic Association, published books, periodicals, films, audiotapes, records, and radio programs. In later years, the ministry also established a Christian leadership training campus in North Carolina. Billy Graham was one of the key founders of *Christianity Today* magazine in 1955, and his organization was highly involved in the World Congress on Evangelism in Berlin in 1966 and the International Congress on World Evangelization in Lausanne in 1974.

Because of extensive media coverage as early as 1949, the name "Billy Graham" became synonymous with the words *evangelical Christian* and *born again*. In spite of inevitable public criticism from those who disagreed with his message or with his association with a wide variety of prominent people, Dr. Graham rarely responded to critics except to reiterate that his primary calling was to preach the gospel.[1] Within the organization of his widespread ministry, he established safeguards against financial and moral wrongdoing. His efforts revealed his strong character, and they paid off. In the words of *TIME* magazine, written when he was eighty years old, "There have been no scandals, financial or sexual, to darken Graham's mission. His sincerity, transparent and convincing, cannot be denied."[2]

Not only has Billy Graham's name become synonymous with American evangelicalism, but it also represents the highest quality of personal Christian character.

Mother Teresa

Mother Teresa never raised her voice. With quiet determination and faultless integrity, this diminutive and homely woman worked to fulfill her vision to assist, in her words, "the poorest of the poor," whom she also called "Christ in a distressing disguise" in Calcutta, India, and many other cities in the world. She founded the Missionaries of Charity, which now has branches in many countries in Asia, Africa, Australia, Europe, Latin America, and North America. The Missionaries of Charity operate hospices for the dying and care facilities for disabled people, the aged, the blind, alcoholics, and refugees from wars, epidemics, natural disasters, and famines.

In world opinion, Mother Teresa's status is unrivaled. She was awarded the Nobel Peace Prize in 1979 and also received other major prizes and honors over her long life. She died in 1997 at the age of eighty-seven, but her work goes on.

In her own opinion, Mother Teresa was a simple nun with a single-minded vision. To her, reflecting the character of Christ was of central importance. She commonly told her followers, "We are called not to be successful, but to be faithful."[3]

Corrie ten Boom

To stand strong in God's Spirit, I don't believe that you have to be a fire-breathing evangelist, a pastor, or a gifted teacher. In fact, God may prefer to use an ordinary person who combines a willing spirit with mature character, someone such as Corrie ten Boom.

During World War II, Corrie ten Boom's family home in the Netherlands became a hiding place for Jewish fugitives who were being hunted down by the Nazis. Corrie, her sister Betsie, and their father were courageously willing to suffer imprisonment, abuse, and death, if necessary, in order to protect as many Jews as they could from the same fate.

Eventually, they were arrested. Corrie and Betsie spent ten months in three different prisons, finally being transferred to the infamous death camp Ravensbrück near Berlin, Germany. Life in the camps was almost unbearable, but Corrie and Betsie used their time in the barracks, daily sharing Jesus's love with their fellow prisoners.

Betsie died at Ravensbrück, one of four members of the ten Boom family to die in Nazi prisons, but Corrie came out of the death camp alive. Before she died, Betsie encouraged her sister: "Corrie, your whole life has been a training for the work you are doing here in prison—and for the work you will do afterward."[4] Part of the training for Corrie involved the development of a Christlike character.

At age fifty-three, she began a worldwide ministry that took her into more than sixty countries over the next thirty-three years. She died at the age of ninety-one in California in 1983. The headstone on Corrie's grave reads: "Jesus Is Victor. Corrie ten Boom,

1892–1983." She stood in faith and trusted her heavenly Father to see her through.

APPOINTED, ANOINTED, AND EQUIPPED

Godly character is one of the most important pieces of equipment any Christian can have. For that reason, God is always finding ways to make improvements in your own character.

First, He has given you His Word, the Bible, so you can understand and receive from Him. He sends good teaching and preaching your way. He puts you with other believers, both weak ones and strong ones, so you don't have to grow all by yourself. And as you pray and seek His face, He sometimes speaks directly to your spirit.

Besides helping you to understand things, God also provides you with real-life experiences that end up being a little bit like the tests you used to take in school. However, He's the most patient teacher you've ever had. He lets you take tests over and over until you finally do pass them. He *wants* you to pass them. His Spirit stays close by to help you do it. As you grow in Him, you learn the truth of the biblical statement, "Our only power and success comes from God" (2 Cor. 3:5, TLB).

God wants you to pass your tests, and He wants to change you—to "upgrade" you—in the process. To change the example to another biblical one, He is pruning you as a vinedresser prunes a vine, so that you will bear more fruit in your life.

"Pruned if you do, and pruned if you don't"

In case you don't realize it already, I need to tell you that there's no escape from the pruning and purification process, although you can fail to appreciate it and cooperate with it. Your best policy will be to cooperate with it. You know what Paul wrote to the church at Ephesus: "You were formerly darkness, but now you are light in the Lord; walk as children of light (for the fruit of the light consists in all goodness and righteousness and truth), *trying to learn what is pleasing to the Lord*" (Eph. 5:8–10, NAS, emphasis added).

As Joyce Meyer says, you will be "pruned if you do, pruned if you don't."[5] Those purifying tests will occur regularly, even if you try to run away from God. But the pruning process will work best if you stay as close to Him as possible.

At the same time, submission to God's pruning and character-building tests does not always guarantee quick results. In fact, part of the testing process itself is sometimes the lengthiness of it. Look at Joseph, for example. The purification process that transformed him from a spoiled, prideful teenager into a mighty ruler of impeccable character lasted for years and decades. The song of his life had multiple verses and repeated refrains. His story has provided us with a wonderful example of God's pruning process. In Joseph's life story, we see how someone can be appointed, anointed, and equipped. Here is a summary of it from pastor and Bible teacher R. T. Kendall:

> There was nothing wrong with Joseph's gift [of dream interpretation], but there was a lot wrong with Joseph. Joseph wasn't ready to use that gift; he abused the grace that accompanied it by deliberately exalting himself over his brothers. It would be a long time before Joseph could be trusted with that gift. In the meantime God, who earmarked Joseph for greatness one day, also earmarked him for a long, hard era of preparation. The Bible calls this "chastening" (KJV), or being "disciplined" (Heb. 12:6). This word comes from a Greek word that means "enforced learning." God has a way of teaching us a lesson. Joseph needed to be humbled.
>
> Joseph's anointing, or grace-gift, needed to be refined. He needed an equal amount of grace on his gift.[6]

In other words, Joseph needed to have his anointing balanced with godly character. His God-provided character would include the humility, grace, wisdom, and self-control that are necessary to achieve greatness. Joseph was appointed and anointed—and he was equipped for the job.

Now it *is* possible to be anointed and never get anywhere with it, but I don't happen to have any good examples of people like that, because you never hear about them. And you can be anointed and get somewhere with it, and then fall down at the end of your life. Saul is a good example of that, and so is Samson. Or you can be anointed and yet fall down because of a character flaw and still get back up, as David did. David, like Joseph, was appointed, anointed, and equipped by God with godly character. He followed through on things. He was faithful. He listened and obeyed God's voice, even when it was as quiet as the voice of his conscience.

I have found that people want what God *has*, but they don't want to do what God *says*. God promises us the glories and blessings of His whole kingdom—*if* we will become wholly and completely His own. We need to become sensitive to His Spirit inside us. He speaks to us constantly about our shortcomings, but here's the thing—His voice is a quiet one. Oftentimes we fail to hear it because of the hustle and bustle of everyday life. We need to listen to His voice. David got so sensitive to God's Spirit that he could repent within minutes of a bad decision.

Isaiah said, "Purify yourselves, all you who carry…the vessels of the Lord" (Isa. 52:11, TLB). That word *purify* means some serious cleansing. A light rinsing won't do. A once-a-week Sunday cleaning won't be enough. Your flesh has to die daily, because you "learn as you go along what pleases the Lord" (Eph. 5:10, TLB; see also 1 Cor. 15:31). Remember that God is pruning and shaping your character, and it is not always the most fun thing. Wise Solomon admonishes you: "Don't always be trying to get out of doing your duty, even when it's unpleasant" (Eccles. 8:2, TLB).

GODLY CHARACTERISTICS

It is so amusing to see our two girls and their two different personalities. My older daughter, Kaylee, is a Tuttle, just like her dad. When she laughs, she throws her head back, turns blood red, and can hardly catch her breath. Believe me, it's contagious. My youngest daughter, Erica, is definitely a Jacobs. She loves to cut up, have fun, and be silly, but when she is serious, she is *so* serious. Although these two girls are different in those ways, they are alike in other ways. Both of them reflect Jamie and me.

Does God want us to be like Him? Yes and no. He has a few important characteristics that He cannot and will not pass on to us, such as His omniscience (knowing everything) or His omnipresence (being everywhere at once). But He can and will pass on such traits as holiness, faithfulness, love, justice, wisdom, honesty, integrity, peace, and joy.

We are His children, and He wants us to imitate Him, to lay hold of His character traits, to be living examples of the saying "like father, like son." It's because He loves us so much:

> Watch what God does, and then you do it, like children who learn proper behavior from their parents. Mostly what God does is love you. Keep company with him and learn a life of love. Observe how Christ loved us. His love was not cautious but extravagant. He didn't love in order to get something from us but to give everything of himself to us. Love like that.
> —EPHESIANS 5:1–2, THE MESSAGE

Let's look at a few of these godly character traits that the Lord wants us to manifest in our lives.

Holiness. God puts it straight to us: "Be holy because I, the LORD your God, am holy" (Lev. 19:2, NIV). To be holy means to be righteous, to be morally and ethically pure, but it also means something more. It means to be set apart for God's purposes, to be separated from sin because you belong to God's kingdom. God wants to set us apart so much that He states His desire as a command: "*Be* holy." He is always ready to help us as we turn away from sin in obedience to Him.

Holiness is one of the most important character traits we can ever seek, and it embraces most of the others. Holiness has very little to do with education or cultural refinement or physical cleanliness. Holiness is a matter of the heart.

Smith Wigglesworth, who never became a very elegant or cultured man, did everything in his power to become a holy one. He wrote about holiness after a long lifetime of serving God:

> If you open up to [the Lord], he will flood you with his life; but remember that a little bit of sin will spoil a whole life. You can never cleanse sin, you can never purify sin, you can never be strong while in sin, you will never have a vision while in sin. Revelation stops when sin comes in. The human spirit must come to an end, but the spirit of Christ must be alive and active. You must die to the human spirit, and then God will quicken your mortal body and make it alive. "Without holiness no man shall see God" [Heb. 12:14].[7]

I cannot emphasize too much the fact that God Himself makes it possible for us to be holy. God wants us to be holy, so much so that He sent His only Son to die to pay for our sin. And after Jesus arose from the dead, He gave us His Holy Spirit so that we would always have the strength we need to stand strong in holiness.

It seems to me that God is always testing me in this area of being faithful, having godly integrity and godly character. I remember what happened one Christmas. I was shopping at our local mall, and it seemed as if everybody was in a hurry that day, including me. I got in line with the rest of the seemingly hundreds of mostly women to have some gifts wrapped, and I waited in line for at least twenty minutes. When I was the next one in line, and just as I was about to step up to get my turn, another lady (from out of the blue, I tell you) popped right in front of me. I was speechless. I couldn't believe it, and neither could the other people behind me. Every fiber of my flesh wanted to speak up loudly and defiantly and tell this woman what she had done, but my spirit said, "Give preference to one another" (Rom. 12:10, NAS).

Well, I listened to my spirit, and when the lady finally left, the lady behind the counter said to me, "Judy Jacobs, I know who you are. I saw what that lady did to you, and I want you to know that it really touched me for you to show that kind of patience and kindness to her." There were at least two other people standing in that line who echoed her sentiments. I shudder to think what would have happened if I had listened to the flesh and had disappointed these women who were obviously watching my every move.

Faithfulness. Faithfulness involves obedience and some hard work. Faithful obedience is the greatest attribute you will have as a Christian.

Faithfulness is conscientiousness, painstaking conscientiousness, accuracy, and exactness. It is loyalty. In another sense, it is also trustfulness, being full of faith, rock-solid. If you are a faithful person, you are concerned about the way you do things. You will do things properly so the Lord is glorified and the church is edified. You will cover all of the bases that you are responsible for. You will endeavor to do everything right the first time so that there is no question about it. You will stick to your commitments, whether they are fun or not. You will follow through, even if you are the only one left.

A faithful person is conscientious about everything: attitude, life-style, worship, talents, gifts—everything! A faithful person is consistent and stable. Faithful people see themselves as under orders, like servants: "So then, let us [apostles] be looked upon as ministering servants of Christ and stewards (trustees) of the mysteries (the secret purposes) of God. Moreover, it is [essentially] required of stewards that a man should be found faithful [proving himself worthy of trust]" (1 Cor. 4:1–2, AMP).

As you are faithful, God gives increase to you. Do you remember the story about the faithful servants and the unfaithful servant in Matthew 25:21–30? Their master makes a journey into a far country, and he entrusts each of them with a certain amount of money. Two of the servants do business with the money in order to increase it. They have different amounts to work with, just as we have different gifts to work with. But it doesn't matter, because they are faithful to use what they've been entrusted with. The last servant just stuffs his money into a sack and buries it in the ground. He doesn't trust his master, and he doesn't trust anybody else either.

When the master returns, the report from the first two servants pleases him. He rewards them richly. But notice what he says to the third, unfaithful servant. He doesn't say, "No-no, naughty-naughty, you shouldn't have done that." He doesn't even say, "Demote him to kitchen duty." He addresses him as "you wicked, lazy slave" (v. 26, NAS), and he chastises him for not earning anything with the money as the other two did. He takes the money away from him and gives it to one of the others. And then he says—this is supposed to be God speaking here—"Cast out the worthless slave into the outer darkness; in that place there shall be weeping and gnashing of teeth" (v. 30, NAS).

May I submit to you that it *matters* to the Lord how we use what He gives us? He wants us to be faithful with it. This is not a game; it is of dire importance. Whatever you have, God expects you to produce with it, and to do it with faithfulness and consistency. God wants you to be faithful to what you're called to be, faithful where He has put you.

Are you a choir member? Well, then, be faithful to practice, faithful to your church, faithful to your pastor. You are obligated to God and to others to do everything well. It's what you signed up for. You can smile while you sing (even if you don't have the solo), because somebody back there on row 18 is going through a divorce and somebody on row 28 just heard her husband say, "I don't love you anymore." Somebody in the back just lost her baby, and somebody in the front just went bankrupt. It may be your smile, choir member, seeing that glow on your face, that will send a message of God's love straight to that other person's bleeding heart.

You can stick to a commitment whether it's fun or not. Are you married? If you are, surely you could testify that your marriage is not always whistles and bells. Sometimes it's foghorns and sirens! It's not always lovey-dovey, tutti-frutti, glory-story, is it? Marriage takes commitment, consistency, loyalty—and complete faithfulness.

Love. No discussion of godly character is complete without talking about love. God loved us so much that He sent us His only Son. "But God demonstrates His own love toward us, in that while we were yet sinners, Christ died for us" (Rom. 5:8, NAS).

His love is one of God's most fundamental attributes, to the point that John can say, twice for emphasis, "God is love" (1 John 4:8, 16). He goes on to say how that applies to us: "We love, because He first loved us.... This commandment we have from Him, that the one who loves God should love his brother also" (1 John 4:19, 21, NAS).

Our God loves us so much that He continually gives of Himself, and He expects us, by the power of His Spirit, to do the same. The Holy Spirit inspired Paul to write this now-familiar description of what love looks like, "with skin on":

If I speak in the tongues of men and of angels, but have not love, I am a noisy gong or a clanging cymbal. And if I have prophetic powers, and understand all mysteries and all knowledge, and if I have all faith, so as to remove mountains, but have not love, I am nothing. If I give away all I have, and if I deliver my body to be burned, but have not love, I gain nothing.

Love is patient and kind; love is not jealous or boastful; it is not arrogant or rude. Love does not insist on its own way; it is not irritable or resentful; it does not rejoice at wrong, but rejoices in the right. Love bears all things, believes all things, hopes all things, endures all things. Love never ends.... Make love your aim.

—1 Corinthians 13:1–8; 14:1, rsv

As you can see, the little word *love* includes many important elements, such as patience. A patient person doesn't quit. He trusts that, as Ecclesiastes 7:8 says, "better is the end of a thing than the beginning."

Love also includes basic kindness, which is a lot deeper than "nice." The old King James word for it is "lovingkindness," which is often translated as "everlasting love" or "steadfast love." Kind people aren't mean and rude, and they don't waste energy being offended. A loving, patient, and kind person doesn't go around oozing self-importance or self-concern or selfishness ("me...me...my...my...I...I...mine").

If you have the love of God inside of you—and you do have it if you've surrendered your life to Him—you don't make excuses for yourself. You don't say, "Later; not now while I'm still going through some stuff on my own." No excuses will work anyway in God's kingdom. There is always somebody who is hurting worse than you are, and the moment you reach out to them, you will find light and encouragement coming into your life. He's making you into His image more every day. All you have to do is cooperate with Him.

Justice. Our loving God loves justice. The Bible says so: "For the LORD loves justice" (Ps. 37:28, NAS). "He loves righteousness and justice" (Ps. 33:5, NAS). "And the strength of the King loves justice" (Ps. 99:4, NAS).

Justice is part of who God is, and justice becomes part of who you are in Him. He will provide justice for every one of your injustices. By the same token, you can display justice toward others in your own life:

+ Justice from loss—restoring losses
+ Justice from abuse—providing comfort
+ Justice from prejudice—restoring equity, equality before God
+ Justice from wrongs—making them right
+ Justice from fear—changing it to peace
+ Justice from darkness—flooding it with light
+ Justice from loneliness—providing companionship
+ Justice from depression—transforming it into joy

"I will set My justice for a light of the peoples" (Isa. 51:4, NAS).

God's justice lights the way for us, and His light shows us where to plant our feet. His light is surpassingly brilliant. Standing strong and sure, we are glad to be part of a kingdom where we can tell the difference between black and white.

We don't stand stiffly like grim sentries, though. We grow like stately trees. Justice makes us glad: "Happy are those who observe justice, who do righteousness at all times" (Ps. 106:3, NRSV).

Wisdom. God's character is infused with His wisdom. He wants us to share in His wisdom. He wants us to *ask* for it regularly. Asking once isn't enough. We need a lifelong supply of it: "If any of you is deficient in wisdom, let him ask of the giving God [Who gives] to everyone liberally and ungrudgingly, without reproaching or faultfinding, and it will be given him" (James 1:5, AMP).

There are two kinds of wisdom: earthly wisdom and God's wisdom. God's wisdom is full of His love and all its fruits, just as His love is full of wisdom. In our lives, what used to pass for wisdom looks like a pale shadow compared to God's magnificent wisdom. He can turn the knowledge that is in your mind as a workman sharpens a tool on a lathe, and it can come out as wise as Solomon.

> Who is wise and understanding among you? Show by your good life that your works are done with gentleness born of wisdom. But if you have bitter envy and selfish ambition in your hearts, do not be boastful and false to the truth. Such wisdom does not come down from above, but is earthly, unspiritual, devilish. For where there is envy and selfish ambition, there will also be disorder and wickedness of every kind. But the wisdom from above is first pure, then peaceable, gentle, willing to yield, full of mercy and good fruits, without a trace of partiality or hypocrisy.
>
> —James 3:13–17, nrsv

Honesty and integrity. In His wisdom and justice, God the Father possesses a faultless sense of what is true, and He never wavers from it. Jesus said, "I am the way, the *truth*, and the life" (John 14:6, emphasis added). The Son has bequeathed to us a taste for the truth. His Spirit keeps us (through the operation of our consciences) honest and consistent.

As you grow in godly character, you will become more and more of a stickler for the honest truth. You will be careful with it, because you will know how easily truth can be twisted. You will raise your children to be honest, and you will conduct your affairs with complete integrity. People will be able to trust you.

You will find that confidence and truth walk hand in hand. You will *enjoy* being open and honest. You will be delighted to discover that you can now pass tests of character that used to make you stumble.

Besides, your honesty, truthfulness, and integrity will make your life a lot easier. As Mark Twain observed, "If you tell the truth you don't have to remember anything"—you won't have to keep track of your white lies (or whoppers) or worry about keeping people happy. You have only one to please now.

At the beginning of this chapter, I quoted Psalm 25:21, "Assign me Godliness and Integrity as my bodyguards" (TLB). Your God-given integrity—your unfailing consistency in following the truth of every matter, great or small—will be your rear guard for as long as you live on Earth. It will protect you from the enemy, who lurks around just waiting for you to stumble. It will help you to make straight paths for your feet to walk and stand on.

Peace and joy. Peace and gentleness and patience and trustfulness are all bundled together with joy. Paul pulled them all into a few sentences of his letter to the Philippian church:

> Rejoice in the Lord always; again I will say, Rejoice. Let your gentleness be known to everyone. The Lord is near. Do not worry about anything, but in everything by prayer and supplication with thanksgiving let your requests be made known to God. And the peace of God, which surpasses all understanding, will guard your hearts and your minds in Christ Jesus.
>
> Finally, beloved, whatever is true, whatever is honorable, whatever is just, whatever is pure, whatever is pleasing, whatever is commendable, if there is any excellence and if there is anything worthy of praise, think about these things. Keep on doing the things that you have learned and received and heard and seen in me, and the God of peace will be with you.
>
> —PHILIPPIANS 4:4–9, NRSV

Paul was telling the Philippians to rejoice—just *do* it—because the Lord is taking care of all the worrisome details of life. If we will trustfully accept the fact that we belong to Him, submitting our every concern to His care, we will find a depth of peace that simply does not exist apart from God.

Have you tasted that peace that passes understanding? Do you know what I mean? The longer we live in the Lord, the more of it we're supposed to have. Paul's advice is the best you'll ever hear: Just take every one of your anxieties and make them into prayers, with gratitude that you belong to a Lord who wants to take care of them, and then you will find His peace. Keep thinking about the *good* things and keep obeying God, and your joy-filled peace will become permanent.

God's peace will set you apart from other people. They will wonder how you can stay so calm and so stable in the midst of turmoil. You will be amazed yourself at how much more effectively you will be able to function. Joyce Meyer says that this kind of calm stability releases ability:

> It is easy to trust God when things are going good. But when things are going bad and we decide to trust God, that is when we develop character.
>
> And the more character we develop, the more our ability can be released. That is why I say that *stability releases ability.*
>
> The more stable we become, the more our ability is going to be released because the potential in us now has some character to carry it.
>
> A lot of people have gifts that can take them places where their character cannot keep them. Gifts are *given,* but character is *developed.*[8]

You shouldn't be surprised that you're supposed to have peacefulness built into your character. After all, God Himself is an immovable rock, a strong tower. Nothing perturbs Him. You can stand strong in Him, and the ground will not move beneath your feet.

"The God of peace be with you all. Amen" (Rom. 15:33).

ALWAYS GROWING

You and I will never "arrive" at a final stage of maturity while we're on this earth. Our God is so much bigger than we are. Belonging to Him means we are always growing into His likeness, always learning, always improving.

The rewards are rich. Your walk with Christ transforms you into the person you always wanted to be, someone whose God-given individuality is fully integrated with godly qualities of character. Much to your delight, you grow into a vessel fit for your Master's use, one who is thoroughly blessed and a true saint.

> But in a great house there are not only vessels of gold and of silver, but also of wood and of earth; and some to honour, and some to dishonour. If a man therefore purge himself from these, he shall be a vessel unto honour, sanctified, and meet for the master's use, and prepared unto every good work.
>
> —2 TIMOTHY 2:20–21

Let God invest Himself in you. Obey Him. Let Him fill you with His goodness. Balance your anointed calling with ever-growing, godly character traits, and then when you meet your Lord face-to-face, you *will* hear, "Well done, thou good and faithful servant" (Matt. 25:21, 23). "When the Lord comes, he will turn on the light so that everyone can see exactly what each one of us is really like, deep down in our hearts.... At that time God will give to each one whatever praise is coming to him" (1 Cor. 4:5, TLB).

And from the days of John the Baptist until now the kingdom of heaven suffereth violence, and the violent take it by force.

—MATTHEW 11:12

The God of peace will soon crush Satan under your feet.

—ROMANS 16:20, TLB

CHAPTER 7

VIOLENT IN YOUR FAITH

FAITH sounds like a nice word, doesn't it? We talk about "faith, hope, and charity." We even use "Faith" as a name for sweet baby girls.

But you know what? For your faith to be any good at all, it has to be heavy-duty. There has to be nothing weak about it. Your faith must be strong—stronger than all of the forces it has to come up against. It needs to be powerful enough to stand strong, and it needs to be violent enough to press forward without getting tired and giving up.

The kingdom of heaven, Jesus told us, "suffers violence" (advances only through pressing forward with forcefulness). As an individual and as a part of the body of Christ, you can only attain the kingdom of God if you participate in its violent advance—by faith.

You have to understand that faith is not the same as common sense. Faith and common sense don't really belong in the same sentence. Not that common sense is a bad thing to have. I hope I have a lot of it. But common sense will never win a spiritual battle. It might even get in your way, because on the spiritual battlefield you might need to do things that don't make one bit of sense to your natural mind.

(Remember what Gideon had to do—using only three hundred of his twenty-two thousand men to win a battle.)

Forceful faith seems unreasonable to most people. They may just write you off. "She's that crazy Christian. She's out of touch with reality." But sometimes you have to get a little crazy in your faith. It's that violent kind of faith that we see in the Bible—in the heroes anyway. It's "confident assurance that something we want is going to happen. It is the certainty that what we hope for is waiting for us, even though we cannot see it up ahead" (Heb. 11:1, TLB). It's the willingness to take risks in order to reach our desired goal. Your strong faith makes you willing and able to press right through the middle of difficulties. In spite of your difficult circumstances, you *know* that you are going to be all right. Faith is rock-sure confidence that what you desire as a child of God is in the bag already. Without a glimmer of doubt, it is *going* to happen. Faith is getting out of the boat when the winds and waves threaten to blow you away.

JESUS, THE FAITH-BUILDER

Real, true, powerful faith is strong because the object of that faith—Jesus Christ Himself—is real, true, and powerful. Jesus Himself showed us personally how to obey the Father and how to take risks of faith.

Think about how He did things. Don't let your familiarity with the Bible accounts blind you to the outlandishness of so many of Jesus's actions. Most of the time, He didn't do things that are safe. Ignoring common sense and ridicule, He braved murderous mobs. He broke the Sabbath. He reached out to fallen women. He seemed to do something different every time. He even walked on water (and so did Peter, at least as long as his faith held out). Jesus topped it off by rising from the dead!

He did these kinds of things because He had come to Earth in order to stand up against all of the evil in the universe. You don't declare war on the powers of evil without the fiercest determination and the most forceful, even violent, faith. Jesus knew things would happen to Him. He knew He would have to suffer in this warfare. He accepted (because of His faith in His Father's perfect will) any amount of discomfort and pain.

You know some of the details: He was born in a borrowed manger, and He knew the stigma of being a kid who was conceived out of wedlock. Here He was, the Son of the living God, but He spent the first three decades of His life toiling in obscurity in the family carpentry business. After He left home to begin to preach and teach, He had "no place to lay his head" (Matt. 8:20; Luke 9:58, NIV). He walked everywhere He went; He missed meals; He got too hot, too cold, dirty, and tired. He was lonely, even in the midst of crowds. He suffered endless public ridicule.

For the sake of His obedient love for His Father, Jesus persevered. His faith did not falter, even in the Garden of Gethsemane when His sweat turned to blood. He went all the way to the cross and paid the ultimate price to achieve the highest goal of all—the salvation of the world.

Jesus had no precedent to follow. There was no *Son of God Tactical Manual.* He had to forge ahead and do everything based on what His Father told Him to do right then and there, disregarding the risks and the difficulty. In other words, Jesus, more than any other person who was ever born, lived totally by faith.

It is this same Jesus who is our Lord and Savior. He is our teacher and our commander in chief. He invites us to join Him in building the kingdom of God on Earth. He is building His church to be like both a family and a militant army of believers who will obey Him and trust Him implicitly, regardless of what He asks them to do.

Your faith-builder

Does the idea of violent faith seem inconceivable to you? Do you more often feel like a wimp than a warrior? Maybe you are sort of hoping that this stuff is just so much hype and you'll never have to embrace it in your own life.

But if you really are supposed to walk in strong faith, where will you get the "gumption to go"? How will you be able to do this faith thing?

The fact is that you don't have to do it all by yourself. Your faith has a focus—Jesus. Jesus leads you, and Jesus is "the author and perfecter of [your] faith" (Heb. 12:2, NAS). Even right this minute, He's at work in you to increase your faith. He may be testing you. He may even seem to have abandoned you. But He never abandons something He's started. He finishes it. Jesus will finish the job of perfecting the faith that He installed in you when you were born again. Paul was confident that He would finish what He started. (See Philippians 1:6.)

Your job description is simple: abide in Him. If you do that, He'll abide in you, and the results will be astounding!

He'll also provide you with specific encouragement along the way, much of which will come in the form of the Word of God, encouragement from somebody, a song, or other things that sometimes will surprise you. One thing is for certain: He will provide victory over the darkness around you. You may have to go through the middle of it before you come out on the other side, but you'll have Him with you the whole way.

Francis Frangipane has some wonderful things to say about the Lord's work of perfecting our faith:

> To perfect faith, God intentionally allows conflicts to storm against our souls. I know we picture Jesus as gently holding us, patting us on the back, saying, "There, there, it'll be all right." Listen, that is not the voice of Jesus; that is the echo of your mother speaking. Thank God for mothers, but Jesus is seeking to get us to stop being such babies. He wants us to grow up into His image.

Remember, I am talking about the real Jesus now, the one who said, "All things are possible to him who believes" (Mark 9:23). If the Jesus you are following is not leading you into the realm of the impossible to make changes in your world, you are probably following the wrong one.

You see, we do a disservice to people when we tell them, "Give your life to the Lord and He will keep you from trouble." That is not true. We would be more honest to say, "Give your life to Christ, and He will empower you to overcome trouble and adversity." Yes, He will take care of you. But He will not do so by putting you in a harmless world void of problems; rather, He will perfect virtue in you by developing character and by requiring faith—all of which creates the spiritual shelter of a transformed life.[1]

TAKE IT BY FORCE

Jesus is the One who uttered those words quoted in the Book of Matthew: "And from the days of John the Baptist until now the kingdom of heaven suffereth violence, and the violent take it by force" (Matt. 11:12). And He knew what He was talking about.

The Greek word for "suffer violence" is *biazo*, and it means "to force," or in the King James Version, "to press." The picture is of someone forcefully taking back something that has been stolen from him. Jesus is saying that the kingdom of God has been and still is forcefully taking back what has been stolen from it, and the "violent" (*biastes*—that's us) are the ones doing it.

We have been incorporated into God's kingdom, so we need to act like citizens of the kingdom. It may take a little getting used to, but that's the way things are done in this kingdom. We need to "stir ourselves up," as Paul told Timothy (2 Tim. 1:6). We need to get some righteous indignation going. We need to get a little more aggressive in the way we act out our faith.

We need to catch the spirit of one of my nieces, who once provided me with a great example of the *biastes* in action. My little niece, Hannah, was three years old at the time, and she had two older brothers, who were ten and twelve years old. My husband and I were visiting their family in North Carolina.

Now Hannah had a doll that was her very favorite possession. Her parents had given it to her when she was just a baby, and she was really attached to it. It wasn't much of a beauty. In fact, this was one *ugly* doll. But you have to understand it was her favorite doll, in spite of its matted hair and coloring marks all over its body. This particular day, Hannah was just playing with her doll in the room where her family and other relatives were enjoying each other's company.

Brothers being what they are, all of a sudden ten-year-old Matthew came over with a mischievous snicker and snatched away Hannah's doll. He ran off to one side, and then he tossed it across the room to his twelve-year-old brother Jamie. The two boys tossed that poor dolly back and forth, waiting each time to throw it until just before their weeping little sister could catch up with them. She was in a tizzy, crying and running back and forth.

Now the boys were having a blast. They thought this was the funniest thing that had happened all day. But little Hannah was upset. She was crying to her mommy, "Mommy! I want my doll! Gimme my doll! Mommy, tell these boys! Mommy, I want my doll back!" Back and forth they kept going.

Then, all of a sudden, something came over that little three-year-old. I had never seen it happen to anybody so clearly. It was as if a light bulb had popped on, and she suddenly realized, "Wait just one minute! That is *my* doll. My mommy and daddy bought that doll for me. It belongs to me. It is mine. These boys have no right. That is mine. They are teasing me. They have no right!" Instantly Hannah stopped crying, and she got this *look* on her face. Everybody in the room saw it, and we sort of stood at attention. She walked over to where Matthew was and she looked right up at him and she shouted, "GIVE ME MY DOLL!"

That little girl got her doll back.

That's the way we have to get before we can take back whatever the devil has stolen from us. We have to get exasperated. We have to recognize the facts of the matter: "That thing is *mine* because I'm a child of God. And you, devil, need to get your hands off it. Now."

When you get the aggressive faith of the *biastes*, it shows. Even the devil has to take note of it. That thing is yours, not his. It has *your* name on it! It's precious and holy in your sight and you love it and God Himself gave it to you. For a while, your life may be tossed and turned. But when you get that *look* in your eye, the devil's fun is over with. He's been having a blast taunting you. The demons that have been assigned to your home, your marriage, your children, your health, or whatever have been having a blast.

But now you turn around and say, "Wait just one minute. Hold on a second. Devil, let me tell you...that is *my* marriage. That is *my* child. In the name of Jesus, get your hands off!" You take it back by force! That's what you do. The violent take it by force.

You don't take it back by negotiation.

You don't get it back because you are so *nice*. ("Uh, excuse me, Satan, uh, I was just wondering if you could maybe give that thing back to me please.")

There is a look of violent faith, and there is a look of doubt. The devil knows both looks. You don't go up to him acting all scared and sheepish. He will eat you. Spit you out of his mouth. Dig a hole and bury you in it and then stomp on you.

You take it back because you suddenly recognize that you belong to the God of the universe, and that whatever your God has given to you belongs in *your* hands, not in the paws of some wretched demon.

Not in Your Own Strength

You may say, "Well, Judy, that's fine for you to say. I don't have the same powerful personality that you have. You get up there and shout and scream and holler. I guess if I was the devil, I'd run away from you, too!"

Let me tell you, I may have a higher volume setting than you do, but I need just as much supernatural faith as you do. I don't do it in my own strength, and neither should you. It doesn't have anything to do with my personality. I'm simply convinced of the truth of what Jesus said: the violent take the kingdom back by force.

This fight is not for sissies. This fight is for people who are strong in the power of Jesus Christ, who know their God, and who know that He is a God who is able to do far more abundantly than all we can ask or think: "Now unto him that is able to do exceeding abundantly above all that we ask or think, according to the power that worketh in us, unto him be glory in the church by Christ Jesus throughout all ages, world without end. Amen" (Eph. 3:20–21).

The battle is the Lord's, and His power is inside of us. Jesus told His disciples, "Behold, I give unto you power to tread on serpents and scorpions, and over all the power of the enemy: and nothing shall by any means hurt you" (Luke 10:19). Your part is to take hold of that power and use it. You have to get to the same point that little Hannah did, where you have just *had* it up to your eyeballs, and you're not going to take it anymore.

Your personality has nothing to do with it. Your physical or emotional weaknesses have nothing to do with it. It's your faith that matters. And your faith comes straight from God Himself.

Defeating Hodgkin's disease. Once I was asked to visit a beautiful young woman who had been hospitalized after becoming very sick. After several tests were run, it was suspected that she had Hodgkin's disease, a form of cancer.

This young woman had lived for God since she was little. She

126

hadn't hurt a fly in her whole life. She said, "Judy, I just don't understand it. I have always tried to love God and serve Him wholeheartedly." I reminded her of the scripture where the disciples asked Jesus, "'Rabbi, who sinned, this man or his parents, that he should be born blind?' Jesus answered, 'It was neither that this man sinned, nor his parents; but it was in order that the works of God might be displayed in him'" (John 9:2–3, NAS).

I quoted Matthew 11:12, and I told her, "The devil has stolen your health, which was precious to you. But in the name of Jesus, you can take it back. The Word says, 'I will give unto thee the keys of the kingdom of heaven: and whatsoever thou shalt bind on earth shall be bound in heaven: and whatsoever thou shalt loose on earth shall be loosed in heaven' (Matt. 16:19). Let's join hands. Let's pray." (Her immediate family was also around her bed with me.)

As we began to pray, I felt that the Spirit told me, "Judy, tell her to take her health back. Tell *her* to speak to this Hodgkin's disease in her body and command it to go." So I did. She was very weak, but she started off praying.

"Jesus, I love You. I praise You, God. Thank You for dying on the cross for me. Thank You that You paid the price for my healing more than two thousand years ago. I just claim my healing. Hodgkin's disease, you cannot stay in my body—" All of a sudden I saw that same *look* come over her face that I had seen in my three-year-old niece. She began to realize, "Wait a minute. Hold on. This is *my* body. My body is the temple of the Holy Spirit." So she began to say, "Hodgkin's disease, I curse you in the name of Jesus. You *will not* stay in my body. You're going to get out in Jesus's name. Go, go. I am healed!"

She wasn't very loud because she was so weak, but faith was rising up in her. The Bible says that to every man has been given a measure of faith. (See Romans 12:3.) It may be weak faith, small faith, or strong faith, but it is *faith*. The Word also says that one mustard seed of faith can move mountains. (See Matthew 17:20.)

Three days later she went home. They took her to two university hospitals to do more tests and found nothing wrong with her.

That's because she had taken back what the devil had stolen from her. She just spoke the Word: "I am healed, in the name of Jesus. I am whole." She got the *look* in her eye because she realized that all she had to do was claim what was rightfully hers. She realized that if He said it, He will do it; if He spoke it, it will come to pass: "The word is very nigh unto thee, in thy mouth, and in thy heart, that thou mayest do it" (Deut. 30:14). All she had to do was release her God-given faith, open her mouth, and speak the truth.

Sometimes God will require you to do some things that no one else can do for you. You have to go to God for yourself. Sure, get some other believers to believe with you, but for the most part, you are the one who has to open your mouth and declare what the Word says about your situation.

PRESS, PUSH, PURSUE

If you are a man, you may find that you have a natural grasp of this idea of being a spiritual warrior and having aggressive faith.

But what if you're a woman? Despite the fact that I have just used two female examples, does it still seem like the idea of "violent faith" is somehow distasteful? Do you have a hard time picturing yourself wearing a suit of clanking armor?

Well, here's another way to approach it. As a woman, I believe that you will have a natural understanding of the idea of giving birth, which, as you may know, can be a pretty violent activity.

Before a woman gives birth, first she has to persevere through nine long and uncomfortable months of pregnancy. Then, when labor begins, she has to press through increasingly intense and painful contractions until finally the time is right to push that baby out into the world. Victory! And yet her real work is only beginning, because now she has to raise that infant into a full-grown man or woman, and that will take a lot more perseverance and all of her mothering instincts. It seems like a woman's motto is "Press, Push, and Pursue" (and that's one reason I named my annual women's conference, "Press, Push, and Pursue").

While I was on tour promoting my first book, I was being interviewed. The interview was going OK, and then the lady said, "Minister Jacobs, explain to me why you think that we Christians, who serve a God of peace and tranquility, have to get into this fight mode? Is it really necessary to feel that you have to fight all the time and be violent in your faith?"

I replied, "First of all, Paul commands us in 1 Timothy 6:12 to 'fight the good fight of faith.' That means that in this life there is constantly going to be a fight." Then I said, "How many kids do you and your husband have?"

"Three."

"Which one of those children do you forget about every day, saying to yourself, 'I'm not going to think or pray about that one today. Everything will be fine, I'm sure.'"

She shot back, almost offended, "None of them! I pray for each of my children every day!"

So I said, "Exactly! It's a fight every day, a fight for your family, your marriage, your health, your body, your finances, your future, your destiny, and your very existence as a child of God. But it is a good fight because *we win!*"

God wants both men and women to press and pursue Him with all of our hearts. Those things that God wants to be birthed into our spirits will never be born unless and until we press and push into Him. Unless and until we are willing to get out of our comfort zone, out of the place of safety, out of the place of leisure...unless and until we are willing to step out, we'll never see the birth of the thing God wants us to have.

It's as if there are heavenly "birthing techniques," if you will, and we need to learn them in order to cooperate with this process. I like to group them together into four categories:

1. Prayer and fasting

2. Worship and praise

3. Boldness and power

4. Aggressiveness and expectancy

Let's take each of those in turn.

Prayer and fasting. In order to see and have what you have never seen and had before, you have to do what you have never done. Sometimes we have to pray as we've never prayed before. Sometimes the only way to get prayer answered is to pray all night. Sometimes the only way to break through to victory is to fast from food or from something else that would normally consume all your leisure time, so you can tell God, "This is what's important in my life, and I'm seeking You about it."

Whatever you do, do it in obedience. You may not be able to hear the Father's voice clearly, but if you will get still and quiet, "you will hear a Voice behind you say, 'No, this is the way; walk here'" (Isa. 30:21, TLB). As far as you can determine, do what you think He's telling you to do.

On the other side of your obedient faith is a miracle. "The just shall live by faith." (That's in the Bible, word for word, three times: in Romans 1:17, Galatians 3:11, and Hebrews 10:38.)

Worship and praise. One of the best weapons for spiritual warfare is worship. Did you know that you can sing your way to victory? Some will say, "That's just a silly little song," but that simple praise chorus may be a force of destruction to the enemy.

Did you know that you can shout, clap, and stomp your way to victory? People will say that's even sillier. But when the people of God clap their hands, it sounds like thunder in the heavenly realms.

When they stomp their feet and shout, it shakes the foundations of hell, creating large cracks.

> O clap your hands, all ye people; shout unto God with the voice of triumph. For the LORD most high is terrible; he is a great King over all the earth. He shall subdue the people under us, and the nations under our feet. He shall choose our inheritance for us, the excellency of Jacob whom he loved. God is gone up with a shout, the LORD with the sound of a trumpet.
>
> —PSALM 47:1–5

Boldness and power. It may not be the way you were raised, but you can walk in supernatural boldness and power. Pray for that boldness. Pray for others to have it. Pray for a boldness toward heaven and a boldness toward hell. Pray for the boldness you need to tell the devil to get out of your life. Pray for a boldness to testify, to witness, to pray, to work. Pursue boldness, and pursue the power that comes with it. Press into God until you get bold and your prayers carry His authority.

Look around you for examples of people who are already bold and powerful. See if they can mentor you in some way. Look for a mentor who is "real," who knows the cost of the long pursuit, who has pressed through the wilderness. Ask that person to tell you how many times they wanted to give up—no, ask them to tell you how many times they *did* give up. Ask that person, "How many times have you cried yourself to sleep? How many times have you ministered to others when you needed a miracle yourself? How many times have you been ridiculed, criticized?"

You're looking for true boldness and power, and nobody gets that unless they've faced a lot of trials and learned how to press through them in faith.

Aggressiveness and expectancy. Many years ago, world-renowned healing evangelist Oral Roberts coined the phrase, "Expect a miracle." He must have had unction from the Holy Spirit to declare it, because here we are, decades later, still saying it. The Holy Spirit has given me a similar statement—"Expect the unexpected." Expect that, unexpectedly, your miracle will show up at your front door, at your desk, in your church, in your body, in your home—and that things will never be the same again.

Your faith must include a sense of expectancy. Just like a pregnant woman, you have to *expect* something to be born. In order to see your vision and your dream come forth, you have to have an expectant heart and spirit. You must *expect* God to do it, or you will never see it come to pass. "Without faith it is impossible to please him: for he that cometh to God must believe that he is, and that he is a rewarder of them that diligently seek him" (Heb. 11:6). Expect the unexpected! He is a rewarder of those who expect Him to do things.

I think of the story of that dear woman in Matthew 9:20, the woman who had had the issue of blood for twelve long years. She was in pain, and people didn't want her to mingle with them. But she was fired up with a kind of expectation that she had never had before. Jesus was passing by! She had to catch hold of Him. She "said within herself [sometimes you have to talk to yourself], If I may but touch his garment, I shall be whole" (Matt. 9:21).

She overcame all the natural barriers of fear, rejection, and discouragement. She had made up her mind before she left home that she was going to touch Him. She had made up her mind to disregard the disapproval of the people in the crowd, especially the religious people who considered her unclean by their religious laws. She had made up her mind to touch Him, regardless. And she *did*. Instantly—she was completely healed.

In the same way, you have to get past the point of giving up. Don't give up on your husband becoming the priest and prophet of your house. Don't give up on your healing. Don't give up on getting out of debt. Don't give up on losing weight. In prayer and by action, lay hold of what you need, aggressively and with expectancy.

Whether you are a man or a woman, are you *expecting*? Are you expecting to birth the supernatural thing that's in you? Don't allow other people to get in your way. Like a pregnant woman, you have to be the one pressing through to your miracle, not someone else.

Take Hold of What's Under Your Authority in Christ

Too many of us live under a cloud of defeat because we don't realize who we are in Christ. We don't know who we are because we don't know *whose* we are. If we only knew what it means to be a child of the living God, adopted into the family of God with the same privileges as His only Son, Jesus, we'd be able to walk—no, *stride*—forward into spiritual and emotional maturity.

Naturally, the devil does everything possible to blind you to the fact that, because of Jesus, you possess more power than he does. He doesn't want you to lay hold of your rights as a child of God. He knows (he even trembles to hear it) that if you ever "get it" where your kingdom rights are concerned, he is toast. One little word from you can annihilate his agenda "to steal, and to kill, and to destroy" (John 10:10).

David said, "I chased my enemies and caught them; I did not stop until they were conquered. I struck them down so they could not get up; they fell beneath my feet. You have armed me with strength for the battle" (Ps. 18:37–39, NLT).

As you read this book, one thing you need to tell yourself is that God has already armed you with the strength to come out on the other side of this thing. He just had to get you to the walls of Jericho so you could learn how to walk in obedience and learn how to shout until the walls come down! He just had to get you in front of the biggest giant that you have ever faced in order for you to see him fall right before your eyes so you can cut his head off.

Your God can work miracles, and you don't have to wait for the next miracle conference to see it happen in your life. Once you become secure in the knowledge of your true identity in Christ, you can speak life into the situations around you. Look around you and figure out what is under your authority. Even if you're not a leader and you don't have a "ministry," you have an arena of authority. It includes your own body, your own possessions, and your own affairs. Your authority covers your family members. It covers people who serve you and people you serve. You don't have to be a leader with a microphone in your hand to exercise spiritual authority.

The writer of the Book of Hebrews urged people to "remember your leaders, those who spoke to you the word of God; consider the outcome of their way of life, and imitate their faith" (Heb. 13:7, RSV). Can you do that? Can you "imitate" the aggressive faith of the mentors in your life? You have a role to play in the kingdom. You have a spot reserved especially for you. You need to *be* there in that spot, exercising your active faith.

Smith Wigglesworth, who became well known in the early part of the last century for his spiritual authority, recognized the duty and calling of ordinary believers in Christ. He once said:

> There is a power behind the scenes that moves things. God can work in such a marvelous way. I believe we have yet to learn what it would be with a...church...that understood truly the work of intercession. I believe God the Holy Ghost wants to teach us that it is not only the people on the platform who can move things by prayer. You people, the Lord can move things through you. We have to learn the power of the breath of the Holy Ghost. If I am filled with the Holy Ghost, he will formulate the word that will come into my heart. The sound of my voice is only by the breath that goes through it.[2]

Amazingly, even if you are the most insignificant individual on the face of the earth, your briefest word ("Stop!" "Go!" "Come!") can carry immense authority. When you find yourself in a particular place at a particular moment, with a specific word from God in your heart and on your lips, you can change the course of history. Jesus said that there was no one greater than John the Baptist, and yet the least in the kingdom of God is greater than he was. (See Matthew 11:11.)

The Bible says, "We wrestle not against flesh and blood" (Eph. 6:12). You're not wrestling with that son or that daughter, that brother or that sister, that husband or that wife. They have not come against you—Satan has.

You know the great hymn by Martin Luther, "A Mighty Fortress Is Our God." In one of the verses, he wrote:

The Prince of Darkness grim,
We tremble not for him;
His rage we can endure,
For lo, his doom is sure;
One little word shall fell him.[3]

Yours might be the mouth that's supposed to utter that "one little word." I love what my friend Martha Munizzi says: "When you don't know what else to say, say the name of Jesus." You just need to say that one little word. Through the authority of God and His Word, you have more power in your little finger than Satan has in the whole wide world. Use it!

WILLING TO SUFFER

You also need to be willing to suffer. As you have probably figured out by now, the Christian life is not a cakewalk. Like it or not, you were born into the middle of a war zone.

Think of what it's like for soldiers in a war zone. Sure, they have been equipped with field gear, and they have been trained. They aren't out there milling around aimlessly like a bunch of scared cows. But they are not comfortable. They have to put up with a lot in order to get their job done. In fact, they consider it part of their job to be uncomfortable. When their commanding officer tells them to do something, it doesn't matter if they feel good at the moment or if they are assured of a safe return. They just say, "Yes, sir!" and they do it.

We need a similar willingness to suffer in our spiritual war zone. A willingness to suffer needs to be part of our violent faith. We need to get tough. (Maybe sometimes instead of "Amen," we should say "Hooah!" like the Marines do.)

How do we suffer? Our suffering is not always physical discomfort. I'm thinking of the Gentile woman who came to Jesus on behalf of her daughter:

> A woman from Canaan who was living there came to him, pleading, "Have mercy on me, O Lord, King David's Son! For my daughter has a demon within her, and it torments her constantly."
>
> But Jesus gave her no reply—not even a word. Then his disciples urged him to send her away. "Tell her to get going," they said, "for she is bothering us with all her begging."
>
> Then he said to the woman, "I was sent to help the Jews— the lost sheep of Israel—not the Gentiles."
>
> But she came and worshiped him and pled again, "Sir, help me!"
>
> "It doesn't seem right to take bread from the children and throw it to the dogs," he said.
>
> "Yes, it is!" she replied, "for even the puppies beneath the table are permitted to eat the crumbs that fall."
>
> "Woman," Jesus told her, "your faith is large, and your request is granted." And her daughter was healed right then.
>
> —MATTHEW 15:22–28, TLB

To me, this is one of the most fascinating stories in the Bible. That woman was an outsider, and she had no one to support her in her plea. And of all things, Jesus ignored her. Have you ever been ignored, maybe in a store, in a restaurant, or in conversation? To ignore someone is extremely rude. Most of us will act like it didn't happen, and we'll keep going even though we're frustrated. But this woman pressed in to what she wanted from the Lord. The cost of her persistent faith was ridicule from the disciples and, at first, complete rejection from the Lord Jesus. She didn't let that stop her. She was desperate. She *knew* she had come to the right place for her daughter's deliverance. Her determined faith won out against all odds, and at the end Jesus marveled at her faith.

When you come up against obstacles, you might just get hurt. There is no guarantee that just because you consider yourself a citizen of the kingdom of God you are exempt from pain. You might make mistakes. But your God wants His kingdom to come—even more than you want it. He is trying to get you closer to Him. It's almost as if He is saying, "How bad do you want it?" One thing is for certain: He will help you endure the suffering that comes with the exercise of your violent faith. He will help you learn new ways of pressing forward.

When my little daughters were learning how to walk, they would call out to me to make sure I'd be there to catch them if they should fall. I would pretend I didn't hear them, yet all the while I kept my eyes on their every move, cheering them on inside as they gained confidence. What a joy it was to see them venture out on their little faith walk all by themselves. Don't you know the Father feels the same way about us when we take faith walks and trust that He knows what He's doing in our lives?

Part of what you are experiencing is that He is making sure that your character is improving steadily. Every time you wrestle in faith, you mature a little more. Remember the various godly character traits that I listed in the previous chapter? They need to keep growing like trees, and your faith is their fertilizer. Let the storms come and let the winds blow. Your roots will just go down deeper as a result of standing strong in the face of opposition.

DILIGENTLY SEEK HIM

Earlier in the chapter, I already mentioned the importance of expectant faith. To underline my point, I quoted Hebrews 11:6: "He that cometh to God must believe that he is, and that he is a rewarder of them that diligently seek him." My point was that God is a rewarder of those who have expectant, aggressive, God-seeking faith.

Now I want to make sure that you understand the importance of *diligence*. Sometimes, like Abraham, David, and Joseph, you have to wait for your promise. You need to press, push, and pursue the God who is your rewarder, because sometimes your reward won't appear overnight. You need to keep fueling the fire of your heart's desire. Otherwise, you will not be able to *diligently* seek Him, you will wear out, and you will fail.

If God rewards those who seek Him with diligence, where are you going to get the fuel to keep going? How are you going to persevere over the long haul? The answer is simple: your diligent perseverance is going to come from your heart's passion for Jesus Christ. You can't handle the pressure unless you are fueled by a hot passion for Him.

You will remember what the Lord said to John about lukewarmness: "So then because thou art lukewarm, and neither cold nor hot, I will spue thee out of my mouth" (Rev. 3:16). He *hates* half-heartedness. He wants *all* of you—body, soul, and spirit—and He wants you to cling to Him as if your life depended on it, which it does. God isn't a rewarder of those who casually or passively seek Him. He desires your wholehearted love, devotion, passion, and commitment.

If your love has grown cold, it's time to do something about it. Get desperate. Repent. Do whatever you have to do to get your passion burning again. If trials and tribulations have worn you out and you have become bitter or discouraged, get some help from godly people and from God Himself. Get past your ungodly reactions to the difficulties that have beset you. Cling to Him. Tell Him, as Jacob did, "Lord, 'I will not let you go, unless you bless me'" (Gen. 32:26, RSV).

Persevere

The enemy of our souls keeps trying to wear us down. He "shall wear out the saints of the most High" (Dan. 7:25). We get so tired of setbacks. We get so weary of delays. Our spirits cry out, "How long, O Lord?" But we don't get an answer to that question.

All we can do is persevere with God's help. As Francis Frangipane writes in his book *This Day We Fight!*:

> The root of the word *persevere* is the word *severe*. We must face the fact that en route to victory our trials may get severe. Likewise, it is with severe faith—severe or extreme steadfastness—that we inherit the promises of God (see Hebrews 10:36). James tells us: "Consider it all joy, my brethren, when you encounter various trials, knowing that the testing of your faith produces endurance. And let endurance have its perfect result, so that you may be perfect and complete, lacking in nothing" (James 1:2–4).[4]

It's difficult, no question about it. But the rewards are truly great. The way stands open before you. It *can* be done. God's grace *is* sufficient.

With David, we can say:

> O Lord, fight those fighting me; declare war on them for their attacks on me. Put on your armor, take your shield and protect me by standing in front. Lift your spear in my defense, for my

pursuers are getting very close. Let me hear you say that you will save me from them.... Blow them away like chaff in the wind—wind sent by the Angel of the Lord.

—PSALM 35:1–3, 5, TLB

With fasting. In all likelihood, you will discover that you need to add some fasting to your persevering prayer. Nothing is more powerful than that combination. Prayer and fasting will make you "more than a conqueror" (Rom. 8:37).

Moreover when ye fast, be not, as the hypocrites, of a sad countenance: for they disfigure their faces, that they may appear unto men to fast. Verily I say unto you, They have their reward. But thou, when thou fastest, anoint thine head, and wash thy face; that thou appear not unto men to fast, but unto thy Father which is in secret: and thy Father, which seeth in secret, shall reward thee openly.

—MATTHEW 6:16–18

Besides adding an element of sacrifice to your prayers, fasting keeps you entirely dependent on God, which is exactly where you want to be. It helps cultivate discipline in your life with the Lord, and it helps to strengthen you on the inside, so you can withstand any kind of pressure that may come your way. You feel weak, which means that He can become strong in your life.

[The Lord] said to me, "My grace is sufficient for you, for power is made perfect in weakness." So, I will boast all the more gladly of my weaknesses, so that the power of Christ may dwell in me. Therefore I am content with weaknesses, insults, hardships, persecutions, and calamities for the sake of Christ; for whenever I am weak, then I am strong.

—2 CORINTHIANS 12:9–10, NRSV

VIOLENT FAITH IN ACTION

Violent faith is active. It is constantly changing and moving according to the tide of the Spirit for a particular time, situation, or circumstance.

Here's what it can look like. Violent faith is:

+ Abraham standing on top of the mountain, with his promise all tied up, holding a dagger up above Isaac's head, getting ready to offer his son as a sacrifice to God in total obedience, so focused that the angel of the Lord had to shout loudly twice, "Abraham! Abraham!" to get his attention (Gen. 22:11).

+ Esther going into the king's chamber without permission, saying, "If I perish, I perish," all for the sake of her people (Esther 4:16).

+ Elijah killing all of Jezebel's prophets on Mt. Carmel after God had sent the fire (1 Kings 18:40).

+ Peter taking the crippled man by the hand, saying, "Silver and gold have I none...in the name of Jesus Christ of Nazareth, rise up and walk," then pulling him up, not knowing what would happen, except that his violent faith made him sure that God would do a miracle (Acts 3:6).

+ Jacob wrestling with the angel, rolling in the dirt, holding on for dear life even as his hip is disjointed, telling him, "I will not let you go until you bless me" (Gen. 32:26, TLB).

Violent faith is what came into my heart several years ago, when I lost my first baby.

Here's the scenario: I was lying in bed, just home from the hospital. I had just gotten out of surgery. Our first baby had died. My dreams, my hopes, my firstfruits—dead.

My husband had brought me into the bedroom and got me onto the bed. I was lying there in pain, despondent, depressed, discouraged, disillusioned, and wondering why in the world this had to happen to *me*. This shouldn't have happened to me! This kind of thing happens to the people we pray for, but it was *me*. I was the one lying there. My husband came and lay down beside me. "Honey, can I do anything?" He wished he could fix it, but he couldn't do a thing. Then he said, "Do you mind if I turn on some Christian television? Maybe somebody's got a word for us."

He turned on the TV, and there was Bishop T. D. Jakes, speaking out these words: "*Somebody* has just turned on this television, and I'm here to tell you that God's got a word for you."

We sprang up—we almost *stood up* in that bed. Bishop Jakes said, "Something inside of you has died. But God sent me here to tell you that death doesn't mean that it's the end. The enemy has said that you will never laugh again, never sing or preach again. You need to tell the devil that he is a liar. Get up off that bed and begin to shout and praise God, for what the enemy meant for bad, God is turning to your good."

I got up off that bed. I wasn't moving around real quick, but I was moving. We began to prophesy to my womb: "Come forth, children! Come forth! Come forth!"

Now fast-forward to the present. They came forth. Two of the loveliest daughters anybody could ever want. God does exceedingly abundantly above and beyond our greatest desire if we exercise aggressive, even violent, faith.

Pressing Past Passivity

Every one of us needs to get used to the idea that this is what the Christian life is about, and each of us needs to press, push, and pursue the fullness of the kingdom of God with the fullest measure of strong faith, violently opposed to the devil.

It's time to press past passivity. It's time to become militant.

It's time to remind yourself that the devil is *not* as strong as God is. He may be referred to as the "Antichrist," but that's not because he's equal to Jesus Christ. He's just "anti," which means "against."

Is the devil omniscient (all-knowing)? No. He'd like you to think he is, and he'd definitely like you to be afraid that he is. But he's not.

Is the devil omnipresent (everywhere at once)? No. He's especially absent wherever God's people are worshiping and loving their Savior. His forces are spread pretty thinly sometimes; his demons are dispatched all over the planet. He doesn't have fresh reinforcements to count on. He just can't cover all the bases.

Is the devil omnipotent (all-powerful)? No, he isn't. But he likes it when people act like he is. The devil said in his heart:

> "I will ascend to heaven; I will raise my throne above the stars of God; I will sit on the mount of assembly on the heights of Zaphon; I will ascend to the tops of the clouds, I will make myself like the Most High."
>
> But you are brought down to Sheol, to the depths of the Pit. Those who see you will stare at you, and ponder over you: "Is this the man who made the earth tremble, who shook kingdoms?"
>
> —Isaiah 14:13–16, nrsv

Is *this* the one who made you tremble with fear? The devil has been trying to fake you out. He has been trying to usurp God's position since before God threw him out of heaven. He knows he is defeated, but he's not going out without a long, hard fight.

So, even though *he* started the fight, and even though you wish you weren't in it, you are. Get up on your feet and fight!

Get ready. It's the season for you to birth the thing that's in you. It's time to press and push against the devil, and it's time to pursue God as you never have before.

> Keep alert, stand firm in your faith, be courageous, be strong.
> —1 CORINTHIANS 16:13, NRSV

> For whatever is born of God is victorious over the world; and this is the victory that conquers the world, even our faith.
> —1 JOHN 5:4, AMP

With God nothing shall be impossible.

—Luke 1:37

Pray at all times and on every occasion in the power of the Holy Spirit. Stay alert and be persistent in your prayers for all Christians everywhere.

—Ephesians 6:18, NLT

CHAPTER 8

PERSISTENT IN YOUR PRAYER

HERE in the United States, if a woman's husband dies, it's sad, but it's not the end of the world for her. She may be quite lonely for a while, and she'll go through a period of adjustment, but she'll get along all right. If she's older, she may have some retirement income, or she may be employed somewhere. She's free to remarry. Whether or not she has family support, there are any number of social services that can give her help if she needs it.

It wasn't like that for widows in early Bible times. There were no pensions or public social services, and, as a rule, women did not have income-producing jobs. In those days to keep from starving to death, a widowed woman was thrown onto the mercy of her family. Her husband's brother was expected to marry her and take her into his home. If he didn't choose to marry her, or if he happened to die, too, then the next brother or next male in the kinship line was supposed to take her in. Her grown children were also obliged to help provide for her. But if that widow had no male kin and no children to support her, she was completely and utterly destitute.

That's the kind of widow Jesus was talking about when He told this story:

Jesus told them a story showing that it was necessary for them to pray consistently and never quit. He said, "There was once a judge in some city who never gave God a thought and cared nothing for people. A widow in that city kept after him: 'My rights are being violated. Protect me!'

"He never gave her the time of day. But after this went on and on he said to himself, 'I care nothing what God thinks, even less what people think. But because this widow won't quit badgering me, I'd better do something and see that she gets justice—otherwise I'm going to end up beaten black-and-blue by her pounding.'"

Then the Master said, "Do you hear what that judge, corrupt as he is, is saying? So what makes you think God won't step in and work justice for his chosen people, who continue to cry out for help? Won't he stick up for them? I assure you, he will. He will not drag his feet. But how much of that kind of persistent faith will the Son of Man find on the earth when he returns?"

—LUKE 18:1–8, THE MESSAGE

What awful thing had happened to her that had made her situation so desperate? We don't know. But evidently it involved an adversary, and evidently the adversary was still alive and kicking. So in the absence of help and protection from a husband or extended family, she was forced to use the only means at her disposal, the local system of justice, to obtain protection from what was threatening her. The only trouble was that the judge in her city couldn't have cared less about this old lady. He didn't care about anybody.

Therefore, she decided she was going to have to force him to act by wearing down his resistance.

She already knew that it would be useless to go straight to her enemy and say, "Hey, knock it off, would you? You are strong, and I am just a poor widow. Go pick on somebody your own size!" That would have been about as useless as it would be for us to go to Satan, who takes horrid pleasure in causing us constant trouble, and ask him to lay off. Why should the enemy respect such a request? It's certainly not in his advantage to do so. He *likes* causing us trouble, and his ultimate goal is to bring us down to hell with him.

The widow knew that the judge was the only person with sufficient authority to make her adversary stop his tormenting behavior. So she went straight to the top. She didn't have any money to bribe him with. She didn't have any social standing. But she had a voice—and a very persistent spirit.

Your voice, you see, represents your authority. Therefore, when you raise your voice, you are releasing your God-given authority over that situation. Jesus told His disciples, "If ye had faith as a grain of mustard seed, ye might *say* unto this sycamine tree, Be thou plucked up by the root, and be thou planted in the sea; and it should obey you" (Luke 17:6, emphasis added). The word *say* is the Greek word *epo*, and it means to bid or command. In other words, it is the opposite of someone who mutters thoughtless nonsense. This kind of speaking carries authority and great conviction. The speaker possesses inner resolve, using his or her God-given *voice* to cause change to happen.

In the widow's case, it didn't matter that the judge was not a model citizen himself. He did possess the requisite authority. That's why she pestered him until he finally gave in. The widow never gave up until she got what she came for. She didn't let anything deter her. She persevered over time and in spite of insults, rejection, and ridicule. She had a clear idea of what she needed—and she had no other options at all.

ARE YOU A PERSISTENT WIDOW?

When it comes down to it, even though you are not that destitute widow, you really have no other options at all, either. If you need healing, you need to go straight to God. The doctors, the hospitals, and the insurance companies are not going to voluntarily reach out to help you. If you need a miracle in your marriage or your family, no amount of money can buy you a solution. You need God to intervene. Even if He uses other people, God is your ultimate provider.

You can't go knock on the devil's door and ask him (even in your best King James English) to leave you alone. He'll act like he didn't even hear you. He has no intention of quitting until your relentless pressure and God's heavenly authority force him out.

But when you stand at the Judge's door, crying out for divine intervention day and night, the enemy gets alarmed. If you do that, he knows, "This one means business!" The devil knows that God has all the authority in the universe. Even so, he won't give up easily, even if the Judge issues a "court order" against him. The enemy will merely shift his tactics. If you're going to be so irritatingly persistent, he's going to get more interested in targeting your *resolve*. If he can wear you down so that you give up your fight, he can resume his crimes against you with renewed venom.

So, besides making sure that you're asking for help from the Judge and not your adversary, the most important thing you can do is to ask, ask, and ask some more, until you have your answer. Keep asking in spite of difficulties or opposition. Persistently ask. Constantly ask. Relentlessly ask. Never stop asking. Your persistent faith *will* be rewarded.

Concerning perseverance in prayer, Jesus said, "Keep on asking, and you will be given what you ask for. Keep on looking, and you will find. Keep on knocking, and the door will be opened. For everyone who asks, receives. Everyone who seeks, finds. And the door is opened to everyone who knocks" (Matt. 7:7–8, NLT). Your adversary, the devil, knows this truth perhaps better than you do. That's why he resists you at every turn. He's afraid that you will get a second wind, and a third one, and will hold on to your pursuit until you win.

Bob Sorge, who knows something about relentless prayer, wrote this in his recent book *Unrelenting Prayer*:

> The enemy knows that if you will just stand there, and never be silent, and never be moved, but lift your voice to your Redeemer until He gets justice for you, eventually something is going to happen. God will inevitably step into action and supernatural power will be released. Divine promises will be fulfilled, and you will be equipped with a testimony that will empower the next generation. In other words, a major setback for Satan.
>
> That's why every device of darkness against your life is focused upon one single issue: To move you from standing before God.[1]

Samuel Chadwick, an English revival preacher who ministered from the late 1800s through the early 1900s, also knew this truth. He wrote: "The one concern of the devil is to keep Christians from praying. He fears nothing from prayerless studies, prayerless work, and prayerless religion. He laughs at our toil, mocks at our wisdom, but trembles when we pray."[2] Corrie ten Boom made a similar comment: "When a Christian shuns fellowship with other Christians, the devil smiles. When he stops studying the Bible, the devil laughs. And when he stops praying, the devil shouts for joy."[3]

Never stop standing in prayer. The devil himself realizes that the one thing that will prevail over him is the prayer of a persistent saint. Jesus declared, "With God nothing shall be impossible" (Luke 1:37). The keyword in that passage is *with*. You can't expect God to just show up and perform a miracle without your help; you have to come into agreement with Him and believe. There has to be a *partnership*, if you will. You have to join yourself *with* God and believe for the impossible to come to pass. He didn't say, "*To* God nothing shall be impossible"; He said, "*With* God nothing shall be impossible."

Keep Standing There

So if you want to make the devil tremble (and eventually give up), just keep standing there before God, asking. Don't be passive or silent about it. Whatever you do, don't give up. Don't take a break. Don't take a vacation from prayer. The Bible declares, "Take no rest, all you who pray, and give God no rest" (Isa. 62:7, TLB).

God is not like the unscrupulous judge in the story. Unlike him, your God loves you and truly wants to intervene on your behalf. David said, "[God]...has an open ear to those who cry to him for justice" (Ps. 9:12, TLB). He may often seem to take His time, but He hears your every cry. He has plenty of good reasons for keeping you standing at His door. Let's look at some examples.

As you stand and pray, you develop more God-pleasing faith. He loves to hear your expressions of trust and concern. To Him, every time you ask proves one more time that you have a heart full of faith toward Him. (If you didn't have any faith, you wouldn't be there for very long.) A heart full of faith is pleasing to God. "The Lord...delights in the prayers of his people" (Prov. 15:8, TLB).

As you stand and pray, you develop more passion. David, who is called "a man after God's own heart," never ceased to pray, day and night. He wrote his desire into Psalm 141:2: "Let my prayer be set forth before thee as incense; and the lifting up of my hands as the evening sacrifice." David had his share of setbacks, but he never stopped actively trusting in God.

For you, as for David, long, consistent, persistent prayers increase your passion for God. If you prayed only one or two times, and your first prayer resulted in a quick answer, you would forget about Him. You would proceed to get as comfortable as you could, and you would stop pressing in for more.

As you stand and pray, you are changed into His likeness. If you prayed only once or twice, the short process wouldn't change you much, if at all. You would stay about the same as you were when you first got down on your knees.

But if you press in to God long and hard, over time you are changed into His image. He too presses in, patiently, persistently, and relentlessly. He certainly doesn't give up. It's part of His character to finish what He starts. He fulfills His promises. He not only wants you to believe that about Him, but He also wants you to be like Him.

He knows that you won't become like Him very fast if you're not under some kind of pressure. Sometimes He lets it become pretty intense. Apparently, it's the only way it will work.

As you stand and pray, you are prepared for obedience. What better place to stay than before God's throne, day and night? When you're there, sustained by the truth of His Word and holding up your hands to Him, you're perfectly positioned to respond to His voice.

He may ask you to do something unusual, as He did with Ananias. One day, Ananias was going about his business in Damascus when the Spirit said, "Go to the street called Straight, and inquire at the house of Judas for a man from Tarsus named Saul, for behold, he is praying, and he has seen in a vision a man named Ananias come in and lay his hands on him, so that he might regain his sight" (Acts 9:11–12, NAS). Ananias could hardly believe it; wasn't this Saul of Tarsus, the guy who had been persecuting the church? But he was used to praying (which involves a lot of listening), and he knew this was what God's voice sounded like. So he went—to the everlasting gratitude of generations of Christians, he went. God wanted to do something through his prayers, and he obeyed.

There are particular things that God wants to birth through *your* prayers. Only you can do it. He needs your voice, your hands and feet, your personality, your everything. You need to be standing in the "volunteer line" when the Master calls you to a prayer mission. The way you stand ready is to keep on persistently praying.

God needs each one of us to do our part to bring His kingdom to pass. No one person can handle all of the assignments; each of us needs to do his or her part. God needs *your* prayers. Nobody else can pray your prayers.

As you stand and pray, you are prepared to receive more. I believe that the Lord enlarges our capacity while we're waiting prayerfully before Him. He wants to give us more than we ever could ask for, "good measure, pressed down, and shaken together, and running over" (Luke 6:38). He wants to give us more than we could have received if we had not endured a long, dry season of waiting.

Sometimes we don't move on to the next level because we don't want to become uncomfortable. That's about the time we stop pressing forward in persistent prayer. It's far better to decide ahead of time that you are going to go all the way with God, stepping outside your comfort zones if necessary. Go all the way with God. Let Him equip you for a greater destiny than you thought possible.

BE THERE

Do you remember the pool of Bethesda (John 5)? The helpless people who needed a healing miracle went there every day to wait for an angel of God to stir the waters, because from time to time, that would happen, and somebody would get healed.

What if somebody decided to skip a day, and that turned out to be the very day the angel came? Those people desperately needed healing, so they never skipped a day. That's why they were there on the day the Son of God Himself came by, and He healed one of the ones who never could have moved fast enough to get into the pool for his miracle.

But the man had to *be there.*

So do you and I. We need to be waiting in expectant, persistent faith so that when it's finally time for our miracle, we're there to receive it!

You do *not* want to miss your moment, do you? You do not want to give up and go home too soon. When the time comes at last, the Lord's victory will be as swift as that healing at Bethesda.

While you are waiting, you may not feel as if you are *doing* enough. Shouldn't you try something different? Perhaps you should try a new prayer posture or fast a little harder or enlist some new prayer warriors.

While you are waiting, in all likelihood you will feel like giving up. After all, if God hasn't answered your prayers by now, it sure doesn't look like He's going to do it. You will think, "It's not reasonable to keep waiting in faith. I'll only be disappointed. I'm beginning to look foolish. I've got better things to do."

However, if you overcome all of those temptations and you stick it out, you will *be there* when He comes. You will see that He wasn't so slow after all. God is never too late.

"I waited patiently for the Lord." In another of his psalms, David wrote these heartfelt words: "I waited patiently for the LORD; he inclined to me and heard my cry. He drew me up from the desolate pit, out of the miry bog, and set my feet upon a rock, making my steps secure" (Ps. 40:1–2, RSV).

Those words might make us think that David found it easier than we do to "wait patiently" for the Lord. But we know quite a bit about David's personality and circumstances.

> When David said he waited "patiently," it does not mean that he was without angst [anxiety]. Nor does it mean that he was always silent, nor passive, nor docile, nor leisurely, nor compliant. It simply means that he looked to God alone and refused to court any other option. It means that he did not lose heart but lifted his cry without ceasing to his Judge.
>
> Look at David's life, and you'll see what it means to wait patiently. You fill your lungs; bring your vocal cords together, let out your cry of anguish and pain; lift your voice

without ceasing to God; find fresh assurance in His Word; breathe in His grace; your soul gently begins to quiet, and you come to a new place of rest; faith is renewed and confidence restored. Then the next day it happens all over again. And the next. In this manner, the soul comes to a new place of resolve every day.[4]

STAND—AND FIGHT!

In chapter 2 I mentioned Joshua and Caleb, who had a "different spirit" from the rest of the Israelites. They were willing to stand firm for forty long years despite negative opinions and many seeming setbacks. They never gave up the idea that God wanted them to conquer the Promised Land.

You remember the story: Joshua and Caleb were two of the scouts who were sent into the land to spy it out. Lo and behold, when they got there, they found a land of "milk and honey"—and they found that the land was inhabited by intimidating giants. All the other spies were scared out of their sandals. They didn't think the people of Israel could make a dent in the giants' defenses. But Joshua and Caleb responded differently. They were ready to fight those giants, the sooner the better.

As it turned out, since they represented the minority opinion, they had to wait forty years to do their fighting, but, amazingly, they had kept the faith so well that they were still primed to fight, even after all those years. Joshua and Caleb exemplify all four key qualities that are necessary to take any promised land:

1. **Sight** (A vision of the land, based on an actual visit and actual sightings from a distance)

2. **Right** (Through Abraham, Isaac, and Jacob, God had promised that He was going to give them the land for posterity.)

3. **Might** (There were six million Israelites who had fled from Pharaoh, and the men were strong and battle-ready.)

4. **Fight** (At first, Joshua and Caleb alone had enough "fight" in them to tackle the impossible situation. The rest of the people had to develop it. The fearful ones who wouldn't fight had to die off before the battle could occur.)

We need to exemplify all four qualities, as well. We need to have the *sight* (a vision for what God wants us to have), the *right* (a grasp of why it is clearly ours to claim), the *might* (a comprehension of the supernatural power that is at our disposal), and the *fight* (a willingness to take on giants, along with an ability to maintain that willingness over the long haul, persevering in prayer until the chosen day finally arrives).

There will always be opposition to your mission. This is nothing new. (Remember the saying, "New levels, new devils"?) Instead of letting fear and doubt and unbelief come over you, you need to develop the fight you need to conquer the giants in the land. The Israelites did it. You can, too.

Get the Vision

You can't ever fight if you don't have the sight first, the vision for what God wants to accomplish. The Word says, "Where there is no vision, the people perish" (Prov. 29:18). This is never truer than when you are undertaking a big prayer assignment. If you don't have a *vision*:

+ Your resolve will dissolve.
+ Your knees will knock.
+ Your hands will droop.
+ Your voice will fail.

A good grip on your vision will enable you to persist for weeks and months and years in prayer.

I love what my friend Tim Storey says: "You've got to trust and go after your God-idea. A good idea may happen, but a God-idea *must* happen."[5] God gives you your God-idea. It's a lot bigger than a good idea. Your God-idea keeps you up at night. It motivates you. Your God-idea and your vision and your dream are one and the same. It's what you have in your heart that you are convinced God wants you to have. You know it's waiting for you. You can see it in your mind's eye. You can practically touch it and taste it and smell it.

You have to keep that vision alive.

The devil doesn't want you to keep it alive at all. He wants to see it dead and buried. Sometimes he prowls around like a wolf, licking his lips. He's after your vision!

How are you going to keep your vision alive, maybe for years on end? Won't it just die of natural causes after too many disappointments? One way to keep your vision alive is to speak to it. Yes, you can speak to your vision and tell it to live, just as Ezekiel spoke to those dry bones (Ezek. 37).

God plunked him down above a whole valley full of dry bones, and He said, "Ezekiel, prophesy!" Ezekiel had a little trouble believing that so much deadness could actually come back to life, but it did—after he spoke to those dead bones and decreed that they should live again.

> He said unto me, Prophesy upon these bones, and say unto them, O ye dry bones, hear the word of the LORD. Thus saith the Lord GOD unto these bones; Behold, I will cause breath to enter into you, and ye shall live: And I will lay sinews upon you, and will bring up flesh upon you, and cover you with skin, and put breath in you, and ye shall live; and ye shall know that I am the LORD. So I prophesied as I was commanded: and as

I prophesied, there was a noise, and behold a shaking, and the bones came together, bone to his bone.

—EZEKIEL 37:4–7

That wasn't all. The vision had not yet come to pass, because the reassembled bones, even though they were starting to look like living people again, did not have life yet. This time, God told Ezekiel to speak to the *wind* and command it to enter the bodies:

And when I beheld, lo, the sinews and the flesh came up upon them, and the skin covered them above: but there was no breath in them. Then said he unto me, Prophesy unto the wind, prophesy, son of man, and say to the wind, Thus saith the Lord GOD; Come from the four winds, O breath, and breathe upon these slain, that they may live. So I prophesied as he commanded me, and the breath came into them, and they lived, and stood up upon their feet, an exceeding great army.

—EZEKIEL 37:8–10

Ezekiel had to speak life to his vision. The whole thing was unreal, like a dream, before he did that. It's the same with you and me. Sometimes we need to speak life to our dreams. Sometimes we need to shout a proclamation and declare a decree—"Marriage, you will *live*, and not die! I'm telling you—get up off that deathbed and start living again!" God gave you that vision, and it needs to stand up and live.

First, your vision needs to stand up on its feet, and then the breath of God needs to enter into it and fulfill it. When God spoke to Gideon and told him to destroy the army, the very next thing the angel did was to breathe into him the breath of God. That's going to happen to you. The wind of God will blow the breath of God into you, and you will be another person. Your part is to persistently, consistently, pray and believe—and, sometimes, talk directly to it. At the end of your pursuit, there is a prize. It may be a baby. It may be a divine restoration or a heavenly intervention. Whatever it is, it's a miracle. It's a breakthrough.

GET INTO THE WORD

Now, because your vision is God's idea in the first place, it must be nourished and kept alive with God's own Word. This is His idea, not yours, so you don't want your prayers to reflect your limited viewpoint or opinions or desires. Every time you ask Him to fulfill your vision, you must base your request on His Word, the Bible.

You need to be in the Word every day. You need to read it, sing it, memorize it, and pray it back to Him. God's Word will not return to Him void—it will accomplish the purposes that it was sent to accomplish. (See Isaiah 55:11.) His Word declares His intentions and shows you how your vision fits in with them. His Word prepares your heart for prayer and furnishes you with the vocabulary to pray with.

In his book *Understanding the Purpose and Power of Prayer*, Myles Munroe says:

> A constant diet of the Word of God will nourish your heart. When you experience troubles, it will be the Word that comes out of your mouth, and you will create what the Word says.
>
> If you confess and hold on to God's truth, you will not be made ashamed. He will answer. (See Romans 10:10–11.) When you stay connected to the Word of God, you will bear fruit in season. (See Psalm 1:1–3.)[6]

It's an irrefutable fact—God cannot lie. Therefore, if He has promised something, it *will* come to pass: "God's words will always prove true and right, no matter who questions them" (Rom. 3:4, TLB).

When you stand in prayer, persistently coming before Him with your request, you are rock-solid sure of His integrity. You are so sure, you won't quit asking until you get His answer. Even if it takes a long time, you'll stay the course, repeating His promise back to Him. If He said it, you know you can stand on it. "God is not a man, that he should lie; neither the son of man, that he should repent: hath he said, and shall he not do it? or hath he spoken, and shall he not make it good?" (Num. 23:19).

When you stand in prayer, you're standing on your God-given vision, and you're agreeing with God about it. Along the way, as you continue to immerse yourself in God's Word, He will convict you and correct you. His Word will keep you on the path of faith so that you can persist in your prayer until the end.

ONE THING THAT'S OK TO GIVE UP

I'm being persistent about this. I keep repeating the same thing— "Never give up. Never give up. Never give up." Pray without ceasing. Be consistent. Be persistent. But I would be remiss if I failed to mention one thing that you *can* give up—food! You can fast. If you combine fasting with your prayers, you will see more results.

I realize that this subject is not popular. Fasting is uncomfortable. It makes you feel downright miserable, to tell the truth. But there's no better way to underline your prayers and put them in boldface print.

In Matthew 6:16, Jesus says, "When ye fast..." Not *if* you fast, but *when* you fast. He assumes that you will do it, and He gives you some suggestions for doing it well.

I wish somebody had given me some pointers before I fasted the first time. At least my desire was sincere, and I have since learned how it works. I was almost twelve years old, and I wanted to be baptized in the Holy Spirit. I had seen my mom and sisters fast for days and days about certain things.

So I up and decided to do it, too. "Mom, I'm going on a week fast," I announced one Monday morning, inspired by one of our knockout services on Sunday night.

My mom—looking back on it, I think her face kind of froze with a little smile on it—said, "That's wonderful, baby. I'll be praying for you today."

"Oh, if you happen to think about me today, that will be OK, but I'll be fine." I was fired up. This whole week, I'd fast. Starting today.

I got to school, and I told all my friends, "I'm fasting today. I'm fasting a whole week. I'm seeking the baptism of the Holy Spirit. I'm going to fast this whole week." My friends didn't know what I meant, so I enlightened them: "I'm going without food. Only thing I'm doing is I'm just drinking water." Their mouths fell wide open.

For the whole first class of the day, I was great. Second period, I was still fired up. At the end of the second period, things started happening in my stomach. Noises were coming from everywhere. Kids were looking at me. My stomach was growling like a wild animal.

Immediately after second period, there was a thirty-minute break where the teachers took us to the gym and we could buy a candy bar, crackers, or a soft drink. Well, I had taken my big, huge Bible with me to school that day, so I found a secluded place and was just reading. "Ye shall receive power, after that the Holy Ghost is come upon you…"

Well, Mary Lonie, the sister one year older than me, came and found me. She leaned down to see what I was reading, and she was eating the biggest Baby Ruth candy bar I had ever seen in my life. In her other hand, she had a big, giant Coke. She put her face right in my face, and she said, "You hungry? You thirsty? How're you doin'?"

"I'm fine. I'm seeking the baptism. I'm fine. Just go over there with your Baby Ruth and your Coke." I got through the break, and I got through third period.

After that came lunch. I went out into the school courtyard and started looking for another secluded place. The air was filled with the wonderful, scrumptious smell that I was very familiar with— fried chicken, my *favorite* food. It was my sister's favorite, too, and in our family of twelve, we never got to have enough of it. Wouldn't you know, my sister found me again. This time, she was ecstatic. With her eyes all bugged out, she said, "Judy, you won't believe what we're having for lunch. Fried chicken! You still fasting?" I couldn't believe she was actually asking me that question. "Would you go through the cafeteria line and get your food and give it to me? Wouldja?"

That's how my whole day went. I got home that afternoon, and my mom said, "How'd the day go?" I burst into tears. She wrapped her arms around me, and I just sat with her on my bed and cried. Mom said, "Judy, it's great for you to fast, and God wants us to spend time alone with Him, fasting at times, but God doesn't expect you to do something that may be beyond where you are in your Christian walk. Just be consistent in your relationship with Him. Seek His face. He'll show you what to do. And He'll give you the baptism, too. "

That's how I learned my first lesson about fasting, which was this: God would rather have you obey Him *daily* than to go on a forty-day fast once a year and forget Him in between. He wants you sensitive daily. He wants you to hear His voice and to be sensitive, balanced, consecrated, and faithful to be in His presence daily.

He also wants you to fast in some way, usually in a variety of ways, consistently. Don't wait for Him to give you a big sign in the sky to tell you to do it. Just do it. You will find that fasting helps you stay right at His feet like Mary, who chose the "better portion." (See Luke 10:40–42.)

"TARRYING"

When I was a small child, I remember being with my mom and older sisters at all-night prayer meetings. I would fall asleep in the pew while they "tarried" in prayer. I didn't really look forward to those meetings. I didn't see the point of them.

However, as I grew older, I began to appreciate what *tarrying* meant. It meant persevering until you broke through to an answer. It meant faithfully staying before God, waiting until He assures you that you have prayed enough. We need to tarry in prayer until we have "prayed through."

There were at least 500 people that started out in the Upper Room waiting for the promise of the Holy Spirit to come, but only 120 tarried until they were endued with power from on high (Luke 24:49; see also Acts 1:4). They stayed there together, the men and all the women, continuing "with one accord in prayer and supplication" (Acts 1:14). When the Holy Spirit came and filled each of them, they ended the prayer meeting and went out to tell the city about God's kingdom.

When you are seeking God about something, you need to tarry, too. You need to pray and pray and pray some more. You need to pursue Him relentlessly, full of faith, until you know He has heard you. You will know when that time comes, because you will feel a certain release in your spirit. You will have a deep peace about whatever it was that you were praying. Suddenly you will *know* everything is going to be all right. You may not have any physical evidence, but you will be able to shift your prayers from tarrying and asking to gratefully thanking God for the answer that you are now so sure of receiving.

Your adversary, the devil, will try to make you want to settle for less than the full answer to your prayers. He will try to wear you down. (I suppose it's his way of tarrying.) But if you hang on to the Word and God's promises, you will outlast him.

Coming Into Your Destiny

In 1 John 3:8, we are told that the reason Jesus Christ came to this world was to destroy the works of the devil. The same disciple, John, recorded these words of Jesus:

> Truly, truly, I say to you, he who believes in Me, the works that I do shall he do also; and greater works than these shall he do; because I go to the Father. And whatever you ask in My

name, that will I do, that the Father may be glorified in the Son. If you ask Me anything in My name, I will do it. If you love Me, you will keep My commandments.

—JOHN 14:12–15, NAS

So Jesus's purpose in coming to Earth was to destroy the works of the devil, and we are supposed to keep on doing the same work He did. We keep on doing it by obeying the Father—and by asking, in Jesus's name, for whatever He tells us we should.

Your destiny is wrapped up in His. It doesn't matter who you are. You are not an accident. Your life has eternal significance. God looked down through the corridors of time and space, and He knew your mother, your grandmother, and your ancestors back ten and twenty generations. He knew what they would have to do and where they would have to go so that you could be brought into existence at exactly the right time. He told Jeremiah, "Before you were born I sanctified you and appointed you as my spokesman to the world" (Jer. 1:5, TLB).

David knew this when he proclaimed:

My frame was not hidden from Thee,
When I was made in secret,
And skillfully wrought in the depths of the earth.
Thine eyes have seen my unformed substance;
And in Thy book they were all written,
The days that were ordained for me,
When as yet there was not one of them.

—PSALM 139:15–16, NAS

David knew that he had a destiny. You have a destiny, too. You have not been abandoned to go through life like a mouse in a maze. Your Father God has a plan for you.

You may wonder sometimes about that plan. You may think there isn't a plan after all. But a metamorphosis is occurring, even as you read this book and continue, faithfully, to stand in your faith. You know how it is with metamorphosis. Who could imagine that an ugly caterpillar could turn into such a lovely butterfly? The two don't resemble each other at all. That caterpillar has a butterfly destiny, that's all. You have a God-destiny, and your prayers will bring it to pass.

You will find that winning through to your destiny involves lots of victory steps. You may pray for a long time before you see each one. Before you receive the Holy Spirit, you may have to tarry, as the disciples did and as I did. You may have to pray persistently and repeatedly before each member of your family comes to the Lord. Along the way, you may have to defeat major illnesses or debt or poverty. You may find that you have been appointed as a watchman on the wall for your church or city or country, and the need for your persistent prayers will never seem to end.

Sometimes you may feel like running away or hiding. But you can't hide from God, and you don't really want to anyway. He holds your destiny in trust. He sees what He has destined you to become through the blood of His Son. He has lined the streets of heaven with the great "cloud of witnesses" (Heb. 12:1), those faithful saints who cheer you on so you won't give up the race in the middle.

God is the One who urges you, as I urge my daughter who is learning how to play the piano, to "practice, practice, practice." He knows that if you don't keep it up, you will forget how to pray just as a child forgets how to play the piano. Paul reiterated the same message. He wanted everyone who read his letters to keep "practicing" in prayer:

> Pray at all times (on every occasion, in every season) in the Spirit, with all [manner of] prayer and entreaty. To that end keep alert and watch with strong purpose and perseverance, interceding in behalf of all the saints (God's consecrated people).
>
> —EPHESIANS 6:18, AMP

Paul also praises the ones who are the most faithful in intercession, such as the faithful Epaphras, "who is one of you, a servant of Christ...always labouring fervently for you in prayers, that you may stand perfect and complete in all the will of God" (Col. 4:12).

Are you ready? What is your prayer assignment right now? Stand before God, day in and day out. Keep living out of your ever-increasing faith. Keep persisting in your faith-filled requests. He hears you. Your day isn't here yet, but He hears you.

Praise ye the LORD. Praise, O ye servants of the LORD, praise the name of the LORD. Blessed be the name of the LORD from this time forth and for evermore. From the rising of the sun unto the going down of the same the LORD's name is to be praised.

—PSALM 113:1–3

The hour is coming, and now is, when the true worshipers will worship the Father in spirit and truth, for such the Father seeks to worship him.

—JOHN 4:23, RSV

CHAPTER 9

CONSISTENT IN YOUR PRAISE

AND WORSHIP

NOT too long ago, I came in from a ministry trip that had lasted for over two weeks straight, covering several time zones and multiple services. To put it lightly, I was exhausted. I got in from that trip in the late afternoon, and my husband said to me, "Honey, I want you to go to our room, get a shower, and go to bed." I thought about how exhausted I felt, how many times I had preached, and how many people I had laid hands on, and I decided to listen to the man of God and take his advice. Especially since he had agreed to take care of the girls.

Just as I laid my head on my pillow and was about to take off into la-la land, I distinctly heard a voice in my spirit saying, "Get up and come be with Me."

My flesh said to my spirit, "That is the devil; I rebuke that voice."

But the Holy Spirit gently nudged me and said, "No, Judy, it's Me. Will you come away and be with Me?" Jesus told us that the spirit is willing, but the flesh is weak (Matt. 26:41), so I spoke to my flesh and told it to be quiet and to line up with the Spirit of God. I got up out of that comfortable bed and began to worship, and the sweetest presence of God infiltrated my spirit and body. When I first got into bed, I had been fidgety, and I couldn't really settle down. But the presence of God gave me such peace, I just fell asleep and slept all night long. I woke up the next morning refreshed and renewed.

People often ask me, "How do you do it? What's your secret? Special nutritional supplements? Do you hire an understudy who looks like your twin?" No. My secret isn't complicated. It is just praise and worship. Praising God and worshiping Him.

I learned a long time ago that praise and worship will take care of anything. When I praise the Lord and worship His holy name, I take my place alongside His angels in heaven. I breathe in that heavenly atmosphere. I get happy in a hurry, even if I started out feeling empty. The Bible says, "The joy of the LORD is your strength" (Neh. 8:10). When I praise the Lord, I step into joy, and joy is my springboard into supernatural strength.

I love to talk about praise and worship. I'm passionate about it. It's not just a secret weapon against discouragement and the devil—it's what I was *created* to do. You were created for praise and worship, too. The longer you and I walk with the Lord, the more passion we will have for Him. And the more passion we have for Him, the more we will bubble over in joyful praise and heartfelt worship. It's supernaturally natural to do so, as the Bible writers attest:

> Let us offer the sacrifice of praise to God continually, that is, the fruit of our lips giving thanks to his name.
>
> —HEBREWS 13:15

> I will bless the LORD at all times: his praise shall continually be in my mouth.
>
> —PSALM 34:1

> Make a joyful noise unto the LORD, all ye lands. Serve the LORD with gladness: come before his presence with singing.

Know ye that the LORD he is God: it is he that hath made us,
and not we ourselves; we are his people, and the sheep of his
pasture. Enter into his gates with thanksgiving, and into his
courts with praise: be thankful unto him, and bless his name.
—PSALM 100:1–4

The twenty-four elders will fall down before Him who sits on
the throne, and will worship Him who lives forever and ever,
and will cast their crowns before the throne, saying, "Worthy
art Thou, our Lord and our God, to receive glory and honor
and power; for Thou didst create all things, and because of
Thy will they existed, and were created."
—REVELATION 4:10–11, NAS

Worship and praise are not exactly the same thing, but they are
both part of the same heart response to the living God.

Worship

Actually, there are twelve different Hebrew and Greek words that
are translated as *worship* in the Bible.[1] All of them portray variations
on the theme: the worshiper bows down in humility, acknowledging
that God is vastly superior and altogether worthy. He lowers his
eyes, bows his head, and bends his knees. The one who worships
may even fall down flat on the ground.

The English word *worship* comes from an old Anglo-Saxon com-
pound word: *weorthscipe* (or worth + ship). The first part of the
word speaks of worth, value, or respect. The second part means to
shape. So when the two parts are combined into *worship*, it means
to shape or build something of worth, value, and respect; the worshiper acknowledges the wonderful superiority of God.

By means of this worship, the worshiper builds an exalted place
for God. "Yet Thou art holy, O Thou who art enthroned upon the
praises of Israel" (Ps. 22:3, NAS). Some translations in other languages emphasize this fact better than our English translations. In

essence, they say, "When we worship God, we build a big throne for God to come and sit on."

That same passage was translated like this in the King James: "But thou art holy, O thou that inhabitest the praises of Israel." When we worship, God comes to *dwell* in the worship we give Him. How about that? The root word in Hebrew for "inhabits" is *yashab*, which means to remain or stay in a place without leaving, to be "married" to it. God inhabits the praises of His people so thoroughly that you can depend on finding Him there. He won't leave an atmosphere of worship. He's a permanent part of it.

Praise

Worship doesn't necessarily have to be showy or loud. Praise, however, is! In the Old Testament, the three main words used for praise are *halal* (implying the making of noise), *yada* (associated with the bodily gestures of praising), and *zamar* (associated with the making of music).[2] In the New Testament, the most common Greek words used for "praise" are the noun *doxa* and the verb *doxazo*, both of which have a strong association with gloriously bright light, splendor, magnificence, and majesty.[3]

Praise "pulls out all the stops." It's active, bright, and loud. You could even describe *praise* as something that's "clamorously foolish." (I know some of you are thinking—"She's talking about herself now.") When you praise God, you turn all the lights on bright, crank up the volume, and express yourself freely. You *boast* about God. You raise your hands in the air. You sing and shout. You want to say more than you have words to express, so when you run out of words, you start to jump and clap and dance. You're noisy. You're all over the place. You make a joyful, uninhibited commotion.

DAVID, THE MODEL WORSHIPER

When David wrote, "Enter into his gates with thanksgiving, and into his courts with praise" (Ps. 100:4), he wanted people to picture a clamorous, loud entrance, with trumpets blaring and too much happening all at once: Fire and smoke. Bright colors and flashing reflections. Lots of people coming together all at the same time.

This was in *church*, in case you missed it.

Even outside the temple, David knew how to throw aside "political correctness" and let it all out. When David danced before the Lord, dressed only in his linen ephod, he looked unbecomingly foolish (at least his wife Michal certainly thought so):

> Now David was clothed with a robe of fine linen with all the Levites who were carrying the ark, and the singers and Chenaniah the leader of the singing with the singers. David also wore an ephod of linen. Thus all Israel brought up the ark of the covenant of the LORD with shouting, and with sound of the horn, with trumpets, with loud-sounding cymbals, with harps and lyres. And it happened when the ark of the covenant of the LORD came to the city of David, that Michal the daughter of Saul looked out of the window, and saw King David leaping and making merry; and she despised him in her heart.
> —1 CHRONICLES 15:27–29, NAS

Michal just didn't get it. She was embarrassed. David was the *king*. Why would he act like that—in front of all those girls?

David knew something that his wife didn't know. He knew that the Lord was better than anything, including decorum. His attitude was "whatever it takes." He said to his wife, "You think that was wild—watch *this*!"

David worshiped like a crazy man. He danced before the Lord with all his might—and we're talking about somebody who was a strong warrior, somebody who had lots of "might." David used his lion-killing, Goliath-stomping, Philistine-slaughtering anointing to worship his God energetically. David didn't care what anybody thought. He forgot about everybody except the Lord God. David knew that God was the audience, not anybody else. Sometimes we have to get crazy in our worship, as David did, to prove that nothing else matters to us but God.

In the pages of the Bible, David is the one who models worship best, because he portrays it in all of its aspects, from clamorous praise to prostrated, humble worship (Ps. 38:6). David learned to worship as a young boy, when he worshiped with his lyre while he was watching his father's sheep. Later, after he grew into increased responsibilities, he was still worshiping, even when he was running from Saul in fear for his life. He praised God wherever he went, whatever his circumstances.

David is held up as a "man after [God's] own heart" (Acts 13:22), and we would do well to imitate him. Since David didn't seem to be inhibited where praise and worship were concerned, neither should we be. Apparently, his methods pleased the One he was worshiping.

Uninhibited

If you have a problem looking foolish in worship, get over it. Get over your concern with impressing that important person in the front row. Don't worry about what people think; worry about what God thinks. Will He be pleased with your worship if it's halfhearted and distracted? Will He like it if you persist in keeping a lid on your heart's passion for Him?

You don't care what people think when you're at a ball game, do you? You act like a crazy person, especially when your team scores. What if you win some big jackpot? Do you put on a blasé face and say calmly, "Oh, how nice." Or when something awful happens, do you just nod your head and act the same as before? If your spouse died, you wouldn't go out golfing on the day of the funeral, would you? In those situations, you would show a little emotion—or a lot. Why? Because we are people of emotion. God made us that way. God wants to stir up some passion in you.

If that passion is buried inside you somewhere, start today to dig it out. Put on some worship music. Raise your hands up to the sky, both of them. Tip back your head and show heaven what your face looks like. Smile. Go ahead; laugh, too! Move around a little. It doesn't matter whether or not you keep time with the music. David said, "Make a joyful noise unto the LORD" (Ps. 100:1). I'm glad he didn't say, "Sing a perfect pitch unto the Lord." All God wants is your uninhibited, abandoned praise. When the music gets reverential, get down on your hands and knees. Show the Lord that you belong to Him, body and soul. Tell Him you'll follow Him all the days of your life. Thank Him for everything you can think of.

Now you're heading in the right direction. Do it again tomorrow. And the next day. And the next.

PRAISING GOD UNTIL THE ANSWER COMES

Now, I don't want you to get the wrong impression. Praise and worship are not like some kind of unhappiness insurance. In fact, sometimes it seems like the more you praise God, the worse things get! There is a definite connection between worship and adversity.

It's not that the worshiping brings on the hard times. But worship does stir up resistance from the devil. And after a while, continued worship drives him out of town. In every situation, God uses the hard times to test and strengthen you. He doesn't send the hard times, but He allows them so that you'll cling to Him all the more. He wants your whole heart, not just in the good times, but also in the bad. He wants you, like His Son Jesus, to learn obedience through what you suffer. (See Hebrews 5:8–9.)

WORSHIP SUBDUES SIN

Sometimes our suffering comes from our own sinfulness. Humble worship is the appropriate response to the conviction of sin. Praise and worship subdue sin and tie it up so that it isn't as strong anymore.

When it comes to personal sin, once again David is a model worshiper. One of the lowest times in his life was the aftermath of his sin with Bathsheba. (See 2 Samuel 12:15.) David committed adultery with her, and then he arranged for her husband to be killed so that his sin wouldn't be found out. Bathsheba had their baby. The prophet Nathan predicted that the baby boy would die, and he did. Then David, putting aside his pride and his sin, "arose from the earth, and washed, and anointed himself, and changed his apparel, and came into the house of the LORD, and worshipped" (2 Sam. 12:20).

Even if your hard time is the result of your own sin, the only valid response you can make to God is obedient worship. You can't worship without repenting, and you can't recover from your sin without worshiping. You need to acknowledge, privately and publicly, that your God is back on the throne of your life. You need His strengthening, and you need the hope that His presence brings.

WORSHIP AS A SACRIFICE

The testimony of Harry and Cheryl Salem is one of the most powerful witnesses of the sacrifice of worship that I have ever heard. Harry grew up in Flint, Michigan. When he was only ten years old, his father died. Cheryl grew up in Mississippi, where she overcame severe injuries from a car accident and also sexual abuse to become Miss America in 1980. After she became Mrs. Harry Salem, she had three children: Harry III, Roman, and Gabrielle. The family traveled and ministered together,* and their youngest, Gabrielle, was just as zealous as her parents in presenting the message of salvation and restoration through music and preaching. Their life was wonderful and fulfilling.

Then, in January of 1999, came a devastating diagnosis: little five-year-old Gabrielle had an inoperable brain tumor. She was not

---

* See www.salemfamilyministries.org

expected to live past her sixth birthday. The next year was a heart-breaking one. Gabrielle continued to travel and minister with her family in spite of her illness. She would even bring her IV onstage with her in a little backpack when she sang. Everyone prayed for her healing. Yet after eleven months, she received her ultimate healing when the Lord took her home.

Even as they said good-bye to their daughter, Cheryl and Harry knew they would need to find a place to praise and worship God through their tears. Benny and Suzanne Hinn invited them to attend an anniversary celebration of his twenty-fifth year in ministry. So one week after Gabrielle's home-going, these two people were found on the front row of a Benny Hinn service, with hands lifted high, worshiping, voices raised in singing praises to God, kneeling and bowing in His presence, a living testimony of "worship as a sacrifice."

Later, Harry and Cheryl wrote a book, *From Mourning to Morning*, about their experience of moving from grief to glory. As their family walked through the valley of the shadow of death, they walked into a deeper, more intimate level of relationship with God, to a level beyond their previous faith, to true *trust* in their heavenly Father. Worshiping Him in the hour of their deepest grief was the key that unlocked that door.

THE COST OF PRAISE AND WORSHIP

The Jews understood the concept of sacrifice. A sacrifice *cost* something, and its costliness made it *worth* something in God's economy.

The Jews had been taught to make literal sacrifices of the firstfruits of their crops and animals. Now, under Jesus's new covenant, believers are supposed to offer the fruit of their lips as a sacrifice; in other words, we offer our praise and worship. The author of the letter to the Hebrews makes this connection when he writes, "Through Him then, let us continually offer up a sacrifice of praise to God, that is, the fruit of lips that give thanks to His name" (Heb. 13:15, NAS).

Even back in the Old Testament, there was a connection between physical sacrifices and spiritual ones, and God commended the spiritual sacrifice of praise more highly than He did the physical ones:

> But I am poor and sorrowful: let thy salvation, O God, set me up on high. I will praise the name of God with a song, and will magnify him with thanksgiving. This also shall please the Lord better than an ox or bullock that hath horns and hoofs. The humble shall see this, and be glad: and your heart shall live that seek God.
>
> —Psalm 69:29–32

When you start to worship and praise, you are making meaningful sacrifices to God, and they are more real to Him than any number of sacrificial animals, birds, or crops. You are touching the unseen reality that is more permanent than the physical reality we live in. Obedient worship, in all its variety of formats, is one of the costliest sacrifices of them all. The prophet Samuel chided King Saul with this truth:

> Samuel said, "Has the Lord as great delight in burnt offerings and sacrifices, as in obedience to the voice of the Lord? Surely, to obey is better than sacrifice, and to heed than the fat of rams.
>
> —1 Samuel 15:22, nrsv

The words *obedient worship* can mean a lot—everything from whether you kneel or stand up during a worship song to your decision about a career direction. When Moses held out his hand over the Red Sea to make it part (Exod. 14:21), his act of obedience was worship. When Elisha left off plowing with his oxen and said good-bye to his parents so that he could follow Elijah (1 Kings 19:20–21), his obedience was another way of saying, "I acknowledge and worship my God by my actions."

Do you see how much more is involved in worship than merely getting worked up in a church service? Worship, what you were created to do, involves every aspect of your life. It's you saying to the devil and anybody else who will listen—"Look, I belong to God, all of me. This proves it." And that releases God to supply all that you need for the battle and beyond.

Remember what Paul wrote to the church in Ephesus: "For we are not fighting against people made of flesh and blood, but against the evil rulers and authorities of the unseen world, against those mighty powers of darkness who rule this world, and against wicked spirits in the heavenly realms" (Eph. 6:12, NLT).

PRAISE IS A WEAPON

Because we are not fighting physical enemies, but rather unseen spiritual ones, we need to use spiritual weapons. Worship and praise are the best weapons in our arsenal. As I have said already, they are sacrificial. At the very least, the sacrifice of praise will cost you your cultivated dignity and your arrogant pride. But it's well worth any cost to see God's kingdom prevail.

Look at what the Bible says about using praise as a weapon:

> Praise the LORD!
> Sing to the Lord a new song, and His praise in the
>   congregation of the godly ones....
> Let them praise His name with dancing;
> Let them sing praises to Him with timbrel and lyre.
> For the LORD takes pleasure in His people;
> He will beautify the afflicted ones with salvation.
>
> Let the godly ones exult in glory;
> Let them sing for joy on their beds.
> Let the high praises of God be in their mouth,
> And a two-edged sword in their hand,
> To execute vengeance on the nations,

And punishment on the peoples;
To bind their kings with chains,
And their nobles with fetters of iron;
To execute on them the judgment written;
This is an honor for all His godly ones.
Praise the LORD!

—PSALM 149:1, 3–9, NAS, EMPHASIS ADDED

Without the "high praises of God," the battle would be lost, no matter how many swords were available. The praise and worship of the saints are what bind the principalities and powers of darkness in chains. Let the anointing of God come! It's time to praise the King! Don't wait for the victory before you praise God. You don't praise God *when* the answer comes; you praise God *until* the answer comes.

Upraised hands

All it takes sometimes is one upraised hand to say it all. The psalmist wrote about the day Moses extended his hand and staff over the Red Sea: "The sea looked, and fled" (Ps. 114:3). The water was afraid of one hand! No wonder the devil doesn't want you to raise your hand in worship and adoration to the King. He knows the moment you do that, you are saying to the forces of darkness, "Flee!"

The upraised or stretched-out hand is a biblical symbol of power and divine authority. Something happens when you lift your hands and voice to praise God when all hell surrounds you. Your upraised hand speaks about what you expect God to do in response to your faith. It says it all. It does your talking for you.

The devil will try to make you reluctant to raise even one hand because it's so offensive to him. The faith-filled gesture of an upraised hand says to him, "You're not on top, you devil. You're under God's feet!"

WHOSE REPORT WILL YOU BELIEVE?

Only by praising God can you affirm that it's *His* report you're going to believe.

Worship is your faith response to God. When you praise and worship, you are telling God, in front of anybody who's watching, that you believe He's bigger than any problem you have. Your praise-filled voice says, "God, Thy kingdom come. I trust You. You always know what You're doing, even if everything around me looks like a disaster area."

Only by worshiping will you:

+ Come out of your grief
+ Get past your disappointments
+ Break the hold of despair
+ Get healed of your sickness
+ Remove your focus from your problems and put it on God

You can keep praising God right through the opposition, because you know that the victory is in the bag already. In fact, the opposition may be one of the best signs of future victory. Jesus had fierce opposition. (Remember His forty days in the wilderness?) Moses and the Israelites had it, too: "Remember what Amalek did to you along the way when you came out from Egypt, how he met you along the way and attacked among you all the stragglers at your rear when you were faint and weary; and he did not fear God" (Deut. 25:17–18, NAS). Amalek's raiders were a *lot* like the devil and his demons, prowling around, trying to pick off the weaker Israelites. "Like a roaring lion your adversary the devil prowls around, looking for someone to devour" (1 Pet. 5:8, NRSV).

As soon as the Amalekites had been defeated, Moses built an altar, which he named *Jehovah Nissi*—"God is my Banner and my Standard": "When the enemy shall come in like a flood, the Spirit of the Lord shall lift up a standard against him" (Isa. 59:19). We need to learn something from that. We need to learn that God is our banner, too. The banner of praise needs to wave in every battle. It guarantees that God will be with you.

God will make sure that you have some firsthand experience. You will learn how to do worship and warfare by being plunged into it, and God will not let you be tested beyond your ability to endure and prevail (1 Cor. 10:13). I'm sure you don't want to escape His custom-designed battle-training process, because I'm sure you want to win!

Tools of Warfare

What are some of the specific tools you can use to defeat the enemy? They involve everything you use to praise God with.

Are you a pianist? Then play that thing, because you're doing battle with it. Are you on the worship team? Then you're on the front line in the battle zone. Worship with all your heart, and do your part to help lead the rest of the people through to victory. You sing that song—it's a tool, too.

If you aren't a musician, use your mouth to worship and pray. Go ahead; clap your hands together. Stomp your feet! Shout to God with a voice of triumph! If you are a giver, give generously through worship. If you have a gift of service and hospitality, do it as unto the Lord, with a joyful heart. When the Spirit of God impresses you to do any of these things, you can be sure that it's effective against the unseen enemy who is lurking all around.

I had a little aunt who is now with the Lord. She was one of many children in my dad's family. She was about three feet tall, but she was a very powerful woman of God. She was one of the greatest worshipers I've ever seen in my life. She would sing with all of her might. She would pray to the highest heaven. She would clap not only during the hymns but also during the choir singing and throughout the worship service, even while the pastor preached, to encourage him.

When Aunt Mary Lee was in the house, everybody knew it, because she always gave 110 percent of everything she had to God.

What works today won't necessarily work tomorrow. Learn a new song to the Lord. Sing in the Spirit. The devil doesn't have any idea what you're saying. Like the old-timers used to do, plead the blood. You know what that does to the devil? It reminds him of the biggest mistake he ever made. He hates to hear you mention the blood of Jesus.

CREATE AN ATMOSPHERE OF PRAISE

I can't ever remember a time when music was not a part of my life. Music has helped me through every trial, and I always turn to it when I am up or down. Now I am teaching my daughters to create an atmosphere of praise with it. We always have Christian music playing in our home. People walk into our house and say, "There's something special about this place. Peaceful. There's peace in this house."

Of course, music can change the atmosphere, but atmosphere can't change your life. I get goose bumps when I go to the Chattanooga symphony and I hear the harmonious sound of all the instruments coming together. I studied voice in college, and I'm an alto. I love it when those altos get up there and begin to belt it out. I just love it. I get teary-eyed every time I sing or hear "The Star-Spangled Banner." It makes me want to stand up and salute, but that's just atmosphere.

Only worship can bring the presence of the Lord, and it's the presence of the Lord that has the power to change our situations. That's the kind of atmosphere I'm talking about. There's something about being in a valley and all of a sudden you open your mouth and begin to give God praise. Your praises will change everything. That atmosphere of praise will make a difference. Remember, God inhabits the praises of His people. That means He's right here, breathing the same air you are, the minute you start to worship Him.

You may say, "Well, Judy, I just don't feel like praising." Then do as David did after the Amalekites stole all of the wives and children out of the encampment while David and his men were off on a raid. (See 1 Samuel 30.) He "encouraged himself in the LORD" (v. 6). Go off somewhere, open your mouth, and begin to give praise to God. You will soon see a difference, and it won't be hard to keep on worshiping until you don't feel like doing anything else.

Praise and worship will hold back the enemy. I'm telling you, the devil is not going to stand around listening to you sing. He's not going to say, "Isn't that pretty? Isn't that sweet? Listen to her praising God like that. How nice." He's not going to stick around at all. To him, it sounds like fingernails screeching down a blackboard. He'll get out of there. He'll stay gone a long time if you keep on walking around, proclaiming the promises and praises of God. If you don't believe me, give it a try!

GOD LOVES MUSIC

Do you know why God loves to hear you sing your praises? It's because God Himself *is* music. He invented it. He understands a lot more about it than the smartest professor at the best music school in the country. And He loves it, in all its variety of expression.

Somebody else understands music, too, and that's Satan. Satan, you will remember, used to be called Lucifer, the angel who was called "the son of the morning." God asked Job, "Who laid [the world's] cornerstone when the morning stars sang together and all the heavenly beings shouted for joy?" (Job 38:6–7, NRSV). Lucifer was the lead singer in heaven when God was creating the world. He was sensational. He was everything you could want in a worship leader, and then some.

Now Satan has taken music and twisted it for his own godless purposes. It's our job to work against that. It's our job to praise God to the fullest extent of our capacity.

DON'T LET SATAN STEAL YOUR PRAISE

One thing that we must keep reminding ourselves over and over again is that the devil wants our praise and worship. The more of our music he steals and the more of our worship he corrupts, the more he captures the joy and strength of God's people, because, remember, the joy of the Lord is our strength. (See Nehemiah 8:10.)

But every time you open your mouth and worship God with a song, you take some of it back! You take back some territory for the kingdom of God. You confuse the enemy. You change the atmosphere, and he can't stand it anymore, so he has to flee. You declare, one more time, that you will not let him steal your praise and worship.

You may think Satan was after your family or your health, but that's not the main thing he wants. The most important thing that Satan is after is your worship. He knows that if he can get that, the rest will fall into his lap in no time.

Beat him at his own game. Fill the atmosphere of your home, your car, and your heart with joyful praise and grateful worship. Keep encouraging yourself in the Lord, and keep encouraging the people around you. Keep submitting your past, present, and future to Him. Keep giving Him your emotions and your intellect. Lay your pride at His feet, and stand up and start dancing with all your might. Worship is like breathing. You were created to do it all the time, consistently. Whether your situation is good or bad, praise the Lord. He is in control, and He loves you.

Therefore, my beloved brethren whom I long to see, my joy and crown, so stand firm in the Lord, my beloved.

—Philippians 4:1, NAS

So, friends, take a firm stand, feet on the ground and head high. Keep a tight grip on what you were taught, whether in personal conversation or by our letter. May Jesus himself and God our Father, who reached out in love and surprised you with gifts of unending help and confidence, put a fresh heart in you, invigorate your work, enliven your speech.

—2 Thessalonians 2:15–17, The Message

CHAPTER 10

HAVING DONE ALL

A WHILE back, I came to a place in my life where I felt I must have more. Naturally, I already knew there was more to life than an eight-to-five job, a house, a car, a couple of kids, a dog and a cat, and renting a movie from Blockbuster every night. I knew there was a lot more to life than looking forward to retiring from it all. I had tasted quite a bit of the new life of the kingdom of God—and yet I wasn't satisfied. I wanted more. More of God. More anointing. More power. More devotion. More fasting. More prayer. More Spirit. More glory. I just had to have *more*.

Do you feel that way, too? Are you beginning to realize that you will not find complete satisfaction in any achievement, any brand-new possession (that car or appliance or whatever you've wanted for as long as you can remember), or any love relationship? Your trophies or your bank account won't satisfy you. Only God can give you peace, joy, and true, deep satisfaction. Only God can take all the bad times and turn them inside out into something new and wonderful. Only God can make your life more interesting and exciting until the day He calls you home.

Divine dissatisfaction. This kind of divine dissatisfaction may be uncomfortable, but it's a good thing to have. It keeps you looking up to heaven, and it keeps you from putting your roots down too deeply into anything else that could take God's place in your life. The only life that's worth living is one that's aiming to be 100 percent sold out to God. Even if you're only 10 percent sold out to God right now, you can increase your percentage. I'm aiming for that 100 percent, because the fact of the matter is that if I don't have Jesus, I don't have a life, and neither do you. We can't find life in a car, in a job, in a bank account, in a husband or a wife, in another husband or wife—it can only be found in Jesus. That is the way the Father has set it up.

As much as I love my husband, there are times when he cannot satisfy me. Even though he means everything to me besides Jesus, and I love him more every day, there are certain times when I have to say, "Honey, I've got to go get alone with God. I've got to get into His presence. I've got to hear from God." My husband can't do that for me.

Look what the Bible says about God's desire to give us a full and satisfying life:

> The Lord will guide you continually, and satisfy your needs in parched places, and make your bones strong; and you shall be like a watered garden, like a spring of water, whose waters never fail.
>
> —ISAIAH 58:11, NRSV

> And my God will fully satisfy every need of yours according to his riches in glory in Christ Jesus.
>
> —PHILIPPIANS 4:19, NRSV

> In Him we live and move and have our being.
>
> —ACTS 17:28, NKJV

He designed us, and only in Him can we find full satisfaction. No substitutes will do.

Divine satisfaction. "In Him we live and move and have our being" (Acts 17:28, NKJV). "Having our being in Him" involves walking obediently in the calling He has put on our lives. "Living in Him" means standing firm in the storms of life and letting Him build godly character in us. "Moving in Him" entails acting with forceful faith, persistent prayer, and consistent worship.

You can't say you are truly standing strong in Him unless all of the components are present and growing stronger all the time. You become more satisfied in the Lord as you stand strong in the level of maturity into which He has brought you.

SIX "STAND STRONG" KEYS

To take stock of how you're doing, you need to look at the components of your maturity in Christ, or, in other words, how strong you're standing.

Go back to Ephesians 6:13 to remind yourself of what it means to stand strong and, "having done all, to stand"—the verse that provided the title of this chapter. Standing strong means you keep growing. If you are standing strong, you will be:

1. Confident in your calling

2. Strong in your adversity

3. Balanced with godly character

4. Violent in your faith

5. Persistent in your prayer

6. Consistent in your praise and worship

Those are the aspects of "standing strong" that I chose to profile, chapter by chapter, in this book. In this last chapter, I want to tie them all back together.

Born to stand strong

My family modeled all of these aspects of standing strong for me as I was growing up. I didn't need a complete explanation of each one. I had living examples in front of me each day, and that's how I learned to stand strong in God.

As I have already mentioned, my mom was a deeply committed woman of God. I am convinced that every demon and devil of hell knew her name—her *first* name. Her mother, my grandmother, was also a mighty woman of God. My grandmother was a lady who helped build churches, and I mean she did physical labor. And she was so chock-full of the power of the Holy Ghost that she could lay hands on the sick and, believe me, they *would* recover.

My mom married my dad, and they proceeded to have twelve children, eight girls and four boys. My dad really had wanted the opposite, eight boys and four girls, so he'd have more help on his farm. So what he did was turn all of us gals into pseudo-tomboys who literally had to do the same labor as our brothers. I was the youngest one.

But the spiritual life of our family didn't depend on how many girls and boys we had. I could see that what was going on in our family went beyond what everybody else was doing. My daddy would rise *early* in the morning to pray. As a farmer, his day had to start early anyway, at five or six o'clock in the morning. That meant that he had to get up an hour or so before that to pray. (He had to get up early enough to cover everybody—twelve kids and later fifty grandkids.) I saw how faithful my parents were to God's call on their lives and to each other. I wanted to be like that, too.

Six of us Jacobs sisters would sing, and our parents would testify and minister to the people. There was a certain point in each service when we would call on our dad to testify. We'd always call on him first, because we knew that if we didn't let him testify first, he'd never get to do it, because Mom was such a fireball, she would just completely take over. She would just come up on the stage, take the microphone out of our hands, and then go out into the audience and begin to preach and lay hands on people. It seemed like she couldn't stop the flow of anointing in her life.

When I was a young girl, she would come into my bedroom at night to pray for me. (She prayed like this for all of her children, but I think I got extra attention because I was the baby.) She would start off praying real softly, just asking God to anoint me and telling the devil he couldn't have any part of my life. Then the power of the Holy Spirit would hit her, and her voice would begin to rise. When the power of God hit Mom, she would shake. If she had her hand on your head, your head would shake. You get the picture. Before her little bedtime prayer was over, she would wake up my three sisters with whom I shared the bedroom.

Later, I'd ask her, "Mom, is there any way you can pray a little quieter? Is it necessary to shake my head that way when you pray?"

She would always respond, "Baby, I can't help it. When the power of God hits me, it just shakes me, and I guess I shake you." She didn't stop doing it, and I thank God she didn't. She was faithful, consistent, hardworking, and loving. Her character was mature. She ministered out of the overflow of her days, and her days were filled with prayer. She would fast for days and weeks on top of her daily routine. She'd be in the fields gathering the crops, feeling very weak because she would have been fasting and praying for her church, for her pastor, for her children.

When my older sisters would come home from school, before they would change their clothes and begin to cook dinner, they would go on their knees and pray. Like our mom, they would fast for days at a time, too. Growing up in that kind of environment made me want to be like them. What it boils down to is that I wanted to exemplify all of those aspects that I have written about in this book.

My family embedded in me a clear concept of what a life lived for God should look like. Everything was all woven together—maturing in being honest, loving, and hardworking, while at the same time consulting God on practically a minute-by-minute basis, praying and acting as He led, worshiping Him in good times and in bad.

Now if that seems like a spotless little journey I've been on, let me be quick to tell you that I've fallen short. There is only one perfect person, and He hung on the cross for us. I've missed the mark. I've fallen on my nose more than once. Those sweet, prayerful, godly sisters and I have had a few spits and spats along the way, but we still love each other. It's just that inside of me, there has been a fire that could not be quenched. I've had a passion and a drive that makes me want to give God a hundred thousand million billion percent of what He has given me. I've wanted to walk with Him, talk with Him, become like Him, work with Him, pray to Him, worship Him, and *stand strong* in Him.

I want you to enjoy those same things.

TRANSFORMATION

I love the scripture that reminds me, "God is at work within you, helping you want to obey him, and then helping you do what he wants" (Phil. 2:13, TLB). The apostle Paul is saying that God wants it more than I do. He's interested in seeing me obey Him and grow to maturity in Him. He knows better than I do how to accomplish this. He knows that first I need to be reborn, and then I need to be remade from the inside. I need to be *transformed* into His likeness.

Our Father God is a good daddy, and He knows that His children need discipline and training. He's going to take us through some things. Yet He knows the end from the beginning, so you and I can be sure that nothing that happens in our lives is a mistake. It may seem like things are out of control, but God has a purpose for allowing them to happen.

First and foremost, He wants to train us to trust Him. He puts His strength inside us so that we have it to work with. He wants us to pass each test more than we want to pass it. He causes our wills to be conformed to His. He lets us choose, but He gives us the information and the freedom to choose His way.

Remember what Paul wrote to the Corinthians: "But we all, with open face beholding as in a glass the glory of the Lord, are *changed* into the same image from glory to glory, even as by the Spirit of the Lord" (2 Cor. 3:18, emphasis added). Other translations of that passage use the phrase "are being *transformed*." In the original Greek, the word was *metamorfo'-o*, from which we get our English word *metamorphosis*.

The Spirit of God is changing us all the time. All the circumstances of our lives are included in the process of transformation. He wants us to be like His Son. He wants us to be able to walk and stand in the strongest faith and the fullest confidence.

Our part is to be willing to step out of the old and to step into the new. Often we need to pray and press in until we obtain the next measure of what God wants to give us. I like to say it this way: "In order to have what you've never had, you've got to do what you've never done." Often, one thing you've never done is simply to stand firm in persistent prayer and bold faith.

I'll use our own ministry as an example of how transformation works. Five or six years ago, our ministry was not widely known. We were doing what God called us to do, but we felt as if we were spinning our wheels. We needed God to open some doors so we could reach more people. We felt we were supposed to have more influence. So we started seeking the Lord. Especially after that bad storm damaged our little office space, we got desperate. We said, "Something has *got* to change!" That was what God wanted to hear.

Now our ministry is growing so fast it's hard to keep on top of it. It has been transformed, and the changes are still happening.

Transformed by the Spirit

Individually, we are transformed into His likeness a little more ("from glory to glory") every time we spend time in His presence. I used to see a dramatic transformation in my mom when she would spend time in prayer. She would go into her prayer chamber with her shoulders drooped, her head down. She may even have been crying, upset about some news she had just heard or burdened down by something that was going on in the family or in the church. She would walk into her prayer chamber with her spirit overwhelmed. Her body language said, "The burden is too heavy for me. I've got to find a place to pour out my moanings and groanings before the Lord."

Sometimes it would be hours before she would come out of that place. But every single time, when she came out, her posture would be different. Her head would be lifted, her shoulders would be back, her hands would be up, and her mouth would be open, declaring the praises of God. She knew that she knew that she knew that things were different, that she had touched God. I saw that happen over and over, sometimes days upon days and weeks upon weeks. You can't spend that much time in God's presence and not come out different.

We can see it all over the place in the New Testament. The fisherman Peter was transformed. He started out as a guy who seemed to have a knack for putting his foot into his mouth. But after the Day of Pentecost, he was transformed. He was filled with the Spirit of God, and he stood up and spoke with boldness: "Men of Judea, and all you who live in Jerusalem" (Acts 2:14, NAS). *Boom! Boom! Boom!* He preached a simple sermon, and three thousand people were added to the church. (See Acts 2:14–41.)

Then in the third chapter of Acts, Peter and John were in the temple, and a lame man asked them for alms. "Then Peter said, Silver and gold have I none; but such as I have give I thee: In the name of Jesus Christ of Nazareth rise up and walk" (Acts 3:6).

In chapter 4, Peter and John are put into jail for preaching in the temple, and five thousand people who heard them preach got saved in the meantime. The next day, they were taken to stand before the rulers, and Peter preached again. The council was amazed, because they recognized that these guys were uneducated nonprofessionals: "Now as they observed the confidence of Peter and John, and understood that they were uneducated and untrained men, they were marveling, and began to recognize them as having been with Jesus" (Acts 4:13, NAS). There was only one explanation for their boldness: they had been changed because they had been with Jesus.

BEFORE AND AFTER

For every kind of change, every "after," there is a "before." Before you had your baby, you were slim. Before you went on that diet, you were heavy. Before you started using that special cream on your face, you had a bad complexion. But *after*, the change is noticeable.

In our walk with the Lord, the "before" and "after" change isn't physical; it's spiritual. Look at how Paul sums it up:

> And you who were once estranged and hostile in mind, doing evil deeds, he has now reconciled in his fleshly body through death, so as to present you holy and blameless and irreproachable before him—provided that you continue securely established and steadfast in the faith, without shifting from the hope promised by the gospel that you heard.
> —COLOSSIANS 1:21–23, NRSV

It's all there—do you see it? Before we met Jesus Christ, we were estranged from God and even unreceptive to Him, doing whatever we wanted to do. After we met Him, He put us on the fast track to heaven and imparted His own holiness to us. We keep growing in Him as we "continue securely established and steadfast in the faith, without shifting"—in other words, as we continue to *stand strong!*

Taking the six aspects of standing strong that I highlighted in the preceding chapters, I'd like to illustrate the "before and after" feature to help you grasp it more personally.

Confident in your calling

Martha Nantoka is a pastor's wife from Malawi. At the present time, she lives in Pennsylvania where her husband is taking advanced training to equip him to return to Africa and teach at a Bible school there. Her husband came to the United States two years before she and their two children did. During those two years, Martha pastored the church in her husband's place, and it grew amazingly.

Then her whole world changed. She moved to the States, and she found the difference between the two countries to be drastic. Here, almost everything was unfamiliar—the fast-paced American culture, the food, the climate, the English language—everything. She felt she had lost everything—her friends, her church, her relatives, and her sense of purpose.

She started praying and seeking the face of God, and the Lord spoke to her and encouraged her with the story of Moses. Moses left Egypt and went to Midian, only to be prepared for a greater mission—to lead the sons of Israel from captivity to the Promised Land.

One day Martha got an announcement about a Rod Parsley conference, and she felt strongly drawn to attend it despite a lack of funds and feeling like such a stranger. I was one of the speakers, and my theme was "stepping into your destiny." She remembers me telling the people: "Move out of your seats. Move into your vision. Start walking. You're stepping into your destiny." When Martha stepped out and began walking, something radical happened inside her spirit. Suddenly she had more excitement, boldness, and purpose, even though she still didn't know what God might be calling her to do. She knew she needed something more, and she knew she needed people to learn from.

Later, she was able to attend my first mentoring institute, where she got the rest of what she needed, even though at first she felt very small and insufficient compared to the roomful of confident, well-dressed American women. She remembers the session when I was speaking about boldness. "Suddenly, boldness just came into me. I was taken out of the pit or the dead place where I had been, and God showed me what to do." In prayer, she had a powerful vision of herself back in Malawi, with thousands of people being saved. Praying further, she heard the Holy Spirit say, "Take the movie *The Passion of the Christ* and show it in all twenty-eight districts of the country."

With confirmation from others and enough funding, Martha went back to Malawi for two and a half months and boldly showed the movie in the marketplaces. More than twenty-five thousand people got saved.

Back in the United States the next year, at another mentoring institute, she heard the Lord say, "You're going to Mozambique," and that's what she did. She returned to Malawi and proceeded to neighboring Mozambique, where she spent four more months showing *The Passion of the Christ* and seeing incredible results, including in one particular area that was well known as a stronghold of evil, witchcraft, spiritism, and ancestor worship. At one of her crusades there, a woman who had not walked for eight years got up, healed, and many other miracles occurred. While she was there, Martha purchased land for a Bible training school, where she and her husband intend to minister in the future. By the time this book is published, she will have been back to Mozambique for another series of crusades. She has been transformed from a quiet, lost-feeling woman in a foreign land to a bold crusader, confident of her calling!

Even if your personal calling from God does not require the same boldness as Martha's does, you need to become confident in your calling, with God's help. If you don't know what He wants you to do, ask Him to show you. He'll give you a vision for what He wants you to do. In addition, He'll give you what I call "the go-ye" or "the gumption to go." This will give you supernatural courage to see the thing through. Somehow, even though you didn't have it before, you will have the courage to face persecution, the fiery furnace, and any lions that the devil might send out against you. You will get a taste of the same courage of those people listed in the Hebrews 11 "Faith Hall of Fame." It didn't matter to those folks whether they were tortured or driven out of town. It didn't even matter to them if they ended up dead or alive. They stood strong in their faith, and they saw their assignments through.

I want to mention one more thing: there's something about *going* in obedience to a word. It seems as if the act of going itself releases more of God's help. When Peter was in prison (Acts 12), the church prayed for him, and an angel came and smote the chains off him and told him to get up and get out of there. The angel didn't transport Peter to get him outside the prison. Peter himself had to do the *going*. He's the one who had to stand up, put on his clothes, sandals, and cloak, and then walk out past the guards and then keep going through the gates. He had to do that in the natural to cooperate with the supernatural miracle that was happening.

Your guidance and vision for your calling and your ability to follow through—they all come straight from God Himself.

Strong in your adversity

You have to look under the surface to see the "before and after" benefits of adversity, because what you see on the surface can actually look worse than it did before. You have to look deeper to see what God has done inside you. The adversities of your life can make you so much stronger in the Spirit that you will truly be transformed. You know what I mean, either because you have already seen God work in your life this way or because you've seen it in someone else's life.

Because of a medical error, Bob Sorge, formerly a successful and gifted worship leader and pastor, has suffered from pain for over a decade, both physical and emotional. He can no longer talk above a whisper, so he can no longer pastor a church or lead worship. But one thing he can do, and by doing it, he has become a closer companion of God and an inspiration to countless people. What can he do? He can *stand strong*. In his words:

> I said to God, "Lord, I've done everything I know to do. I've prayed, I've praised, I've repented, I've fasted, I've rebuked, I've surrendered, I've read books, I've quoted Scriptures, I've spent time in Your presence, I've reconciled with everyone I could conceive had a problem with me, I've gone on an extended personal retreat in solitude. I don't know of anything else to do."
>
> The next morning I awoke and this verse was whispered gently into my heart, "and having done all, to stand" (Ephesians 6:13). I felt like I didn't have strength to do anything else, but yes, I could still stand. People would ask me, "How are you doing?" and my answer was, "Standing."
>
> Some victories are gained not through an aggressive posturing of faith, but by simply standing. God didn't deliver Joseph from his prison because Joseph had a dynamic stance of faith, but because he kept his gaze fixed upon God. Joseph didn't understand what was happening to him. He could get powerful revelations for other people (the butler and the baker), but when it came to his own life he could see nothing. But at the right time God came and delivered him. "The Lord...does not despise His prisoners" (Psalm 69:33).[1]

Far from being a last resort or a last-ditch compensation for repeated failures, standing strong is the *result* of a life lived in and for God. Standing strong keeps Bob—and you and me—right in the middle of the palm of God's hand, no matter what our circumstances are.

Balanced with godly character

Joseph is one of the best biblical examples of "before and after" character development, especially because he grew and matured and stood strong over such a long period of time. He went from being a cocky "daddy's boy" to being a man of mature character. And then there's Jesus Himself, who is certainly our best example of what mature character should look like overall, even though His character didn't have to develop from a low point of immaturity. As we read about Him in the New Testament, we see in Him a picture of perfectly balanced character.

The most remarkable thing about Jesus's character is the way it combined bold action with quiet humility. Jesus wasn't afraid to speak up, and He spoke with authority. (See John 7:46.) His words could sound abrupt and even harsh. (See Mark 7:27.) And yet He could melt a heart with a few words (think of the woman caught in adultery, John 8:10–11), and at what seemed like the perfect time to make some speech in His own defense, He uttered not a word (Matt. 27:12, 14).

Jesus showed us how to stand before persecutors and accusers— with a willingness to suffer and a quiet confidence that could only come from an unshakable faith that His Father was with Him. He "knew what was in man" and He knew His Father's heart and He knew that His assignment would be costly.

Jesus was perfectly "well adjusted," to use the popular term. He demonstrated an amazing array of emotions, but none of them ever got the best of Him. He always showed the right blend of a slow-to-get-angry spirit and righteous fury. He also worked long hours, diligently. (Remember, He was a carpenter for most of His adult years.) And yet He knew how to enjoy a relaxing meal with His friends. He also knew when to retreat from everyone.

When He was faced with arrest, scourging, and crucifixion, His obedience and strength of character enabled Him to keep moving, to not give up, to remain focused on His Father, and yet to take a moment to look after His widowed mother's welfare. His actions said, "I don't want to do this. But I *will* to do it." He was confident that His Father would enable Him to complete His assignment, to fulfill the purpose for which He came to Earth.

Balance. Confidence. Peace. Jesus had it, and He wants to impart it to you and me. He wants us to reflect His single-minded devotion to the Father's will, His courage, His humility. He wants us to grow in holiness, faithfulness, love, wisdom, honesty, integrity, peace, and joy.

God provides us with a lifetime supply of trials and tests to help us grow in character. Look back on your own walk with Him. What character traits has He been working on? Can you see some progress? What is your "growing edge" right now?

Violent in your faith

Jesus is not only your perfect example of character development, but He is also "the author and perfecter" of your faith (Heb. 12:2, NAS). He Himself not only lived by faith from day one, but He also made sure we knew that we are supposed to live that way, too. He told people, simply, "Have faith in God" (Mark 11:22). He commended faith, especially unusually strong faith, wherever he saw it:

> When Jesus heard it, he marvelled, and said to them that followed, Verily I say unto you, I have not found so great faith, no, not in Israel.
>
> —MATTHEW 8:10

> O woman, great is thy faith: be it unto thee even as thou wilt. And her daughter was made whole from that very hour.
>
> —MATTHEW 15:28

> When Jesus saw their faith, he said to the paralytic, "Son, your sins are forgiven."
>
> —MARK 2:5, NRSV

Jesus sometimes got a little exasperated with His disciples for their faltering faith, saying, "Where is your faith?" "Why didn't you have more faith?" "O ye of little faith!" (See Matthew 8:26; 14:31; 16:8; and parallel stories in the other Gospels.) It was as if He felt faith in God was such an *obvious* "given"—why on earth couldn't these people see it?

Of course, Jesus and the Father know full well that we need to grow in our faith, and that's where the "before and after" come in. Before we recognized the importance of faith, we struggled along on our own strength. We thought we could pull it off somehow. Then we began to see a pattern: right in the middle of a hard time, God would send a word or some kind of help. He didn't seem to send it very early in the process. In fact, often, the help came very late, almost at the last minute. What was this about?

It's about growing in your faith-response to Him. It's about putting your faith in *Him* and not in your own capabilities or in the "powers that be." It's about being tested and tried. It's about learning how to live by faith.

In the process of arriving at God's "after" place, the faith of every one of us will be tested. Nothing is impossible to those who believe, but more often than not, we have to go through something the hard way in order to see results. Our faith needs to be vigorous, well trained, "muscular," and, often, violent. We aren't in kindergarten anymore. This is war. We have an enemy, and he hates God with a perfect hatred. As Bob Sorge explains so well:

> He can't get to God directly...so he does the next best thing. He assaults God by attacking you.
>
> The prophet wrote to God's people, "He who touches you touches the apple of His eye'" (Zechariah 2:8). The apple of the eye is another term for the pupil of the eye. The pupil is the most sensitive member of the entire body. We blink involuntarily in the face of danger because the body's first instinc-

tive reflex is to protect the eye. When you get a speck in your eye, the whole universe stops until you get it out. By calling us the pupil of His eye, God was saying He is as protective over us as we are over our eyes. Satan knows that when he strikes us, God takes it in the eye. So he connives ways to inflict maximum damage upon our lives in order to strike at God....

We live in a war zone, and the wise will maintain constant vigilance regarding the wiles of the devil.[2]

We are wrestling against principalities and powers that are challenging our "standing rights." Having lost his own standing before God's throne, the devil wants to get in his last licks, trying to take out as many of God's precious human children as he can. He wants you to become a statistic. Don't let him get you.

Maintain that determined posture. Stand strong in your faith.

Persistent in your prayer

Once you are built up in your faith, what are you going to do? Take a little breather from the warfare? I don't think so.

Some people act like it's just too much trouble to live by faith every day, fighting battles, holding the ground you've won, laying down your own agenda and obeying God's. "Oh, I'm so tired. *Whew.* I've been working so hard to build that thing, and now it's done, and I need a break."

Well, guess who doesn't intend to take a break? The devil and all of his demons. They just love it when one of God's own children decides to take a rest break. That means they can take advantage of some weakness in that person, and they can slide right on in to undermine the latest victory.

It's not for nothing that Paul said, "Pray without ceasing" (1 Thess. 5:17), and Peter advised us, "Keep alert. Like a roaring lion your adversary the devil prowls around, looking for someone to devour.

Resist him, steadfast in your faith" (1 Pet. 5:8–9, NRSV). That's the way it is, and you can't change it. What you *can* do is stand strong.

You don't have to be a lone ranger. That's no way to run a war. God put you in a church so you can work, worship, love, obey, and pray *together*. The kingdom of God is too big for you to comprehend all by yourself. You need to get real good at doing your assigned part, and work and pray alongside others who are also good at their assigned parts. Hook yourself up with a man or woman of God who operates with integrity, who flows in the Spirit, someone who can be a life coach to you. The Bible informs us:

> Two are better than one; because they have a good reward for their labour. For if they fall, the one will lift up his fellow: but woe to him that is alone when he falleth; for he hath not another to help him up. Again, if two lie together, then they have heat: but how can one be warm alone? And if one prevail against him, two shall withstand him; and a threefold cord is not quickly broken.
>
> —ECCLESIASTES 4:9–12

I learned that God doesn't want us standing by ourselves when I was in the third grade. I was small, and I was shy. There was this really big girl in my class who was always picking on me. I would cry on the playground, but I didn't tell anyone about the situation. One day on the bus, my sister Mary Lonie saw me crying. She asked me why, and I proceeded to expose my bully classmate. She said, "Stop crying! I will take care of it tomorrow!" I knew she would.

First thing that next morning, my sister came to my classroom door with two of her buddies. "Which one is it?" she asked me. I pointed to a tall, lanky girl. She said to me, "Go tell her I want to see her outside the door." I did, and this girl very hesitantly walked over to the door where my sisters and her cohorts were waiting. My sister began, "I hear you been picking on my little sister!"

"Yeah!" agreed her two friends.

"And I don't like it!"

"Yeah!" they chorused.

"You'd better leave my little sister alone if you know what's good for you," she threatened, holding up her balled fist.

The other two responded with, you guessed it, "Yeah!"

From that day on, that bully never bothered me again. Why am I sharing this story? Because sometimes you have to get someone to stand strong with you. God gives us brothers and sisters in Christ to help us carry our loads. Silas encouraged Paul; Mark encouraged Barnabas; and Peter, James, and John stood with our Lord. You may need someone to stand with you, too. That's why we need to maintain the unity of the body of Christ.

The enemy wants to scatter us from each other so we can't accomplish God's work. Even if you don't have any visible support, the Father, Son, and Holy Spirit will always go before you, and the angels will always encamp around those who love God. You are not alone—Emmanuel, God with us!

Consistent in your praise and worship

Before you knew about the power of praise and worship, you just coasted along, hoping your road of life would stay relatively smooth. When you hit a pothole and ran into the ditch, you scrambled to get back on your feet and made sure you never hit that particular pothole again. You didn't spend much time thanking God, unless you could tell that it was His hand that had saved you from disaster. You certainly didn't spend much time worshiping Him between disasters, except maybe for a couple of hours on Sunday.

Then came the day when you recognized that all of heaven is one big praise and worship session. It's going on right now, it's been going on for eons, and it will be going on for all eternity. The angels and all the saints, including the ones like you who haven't "graduated" yet to stand before the throne, join their voices to create a noisy cacophony of praise. God's kingdom doesn't run on petroleum or electricity—it runs on *worship*.

After you realized how important worship is and you experienced how the Spirit of God could pump up your lungs to praise, you still tended to forget about it sometimes. You still had some "coasting" times.

I'm here to remind you to get consistent in your praise and worship. It's an important part of your "standing stance." Worship is powerful. Worship is powerful because something happens in the heavenlies when we do it. In the natural, you don't see much. That's why it's so easy to forget about it. But in the supernatural realm, your worship is moving mountains.

It's not because you have a great singing voice (maybe you don't). It's not because you're louder than the person next to you (maybe you are silent today). It's because you're laying your whole being down before the God of the universe, over and over, establishing the fact that He's Lord and you're not. You're exalting the name above all names, the name that makes demons tremble and angels blow their trumpets.

The Standing-Strong Life

Standing strong in Jesus—the standing-strong life is real life. Standing strong in the Spirit is the only way to live. All other ways of life do not deliver the goods as advertised.

Standing strong, deeply rooted in Him, you will grow and thrive. You will fulfill your destiny. Paul prayed for you:

> I pray that, according to the riches of his glory, he may grant that you may be strengthened in your inner being with power through his Spirit, and that Christ may dwell in your hearts through faith, as you are being rooted and grounded in love. I pray that you may have the power to comprehend, with all the saints, what is the breadth and length and height and depth,

and to know the love of Christ that surpasses knowledge, so that you may be filled with all the fullness of God. Now to him who by the power at work within us is able to accomplish abundantly far more than all we can ask or imagine, to him be glory in the church and in Christ Jesus to all generations, forever and ever. Amen.

—EPHESIANS 3:16–21, NRSV

Right now, as you close this book, just as Paul did, I'm praying for you, too. May the Lord make you able to stand strong, right now and for your whole life long, in the faith He so generously supplies. May you be able to reach out and take hold of His provision and obey Him as soon as you hear Him speaking to you. May He encourage you with His presence so that you don't lose heart and throw off His plans for your life. With energy and faith may you walk and run and *stand strong* in the Lord Jesus Christ. In His name, and with rejoicing, amen.

It's not just for your sake that I'm rejoicing. It's for my sake, too. I echo Paul, Silas, and Timothy when they wrote, "It gives us new life, knowing you remain strong in the Lord" (1 Thess. 3:8, NLT). It does. Keep standing strong!

Notes

Chapter 1 • The "Standing Stance"

1. Myles Munroe, *Understanding the Purpose and Power of Prayer: Earthly License for Heavenly Interference* (New Kensington, PA: Whitaker House, 2002), 143.

2. J. Lee Grady, "Secret Agent Man," *Charisma*, March 2005, http://www.charismamag.com/display.php?id=10614 (accessed February 8, 2007).

3. OpenDoorsUSA.org, "Brother Andrew Reflects on 50 Years of Ministry," news release, July 14, 2005, http://www.opendoorsusa.org (accessed February 8, 2007).

4. Ibid.

5. Darlene Bishop, *Your Life Follows Your Words: Releasing the Prayer of Faith* (Denver, CO: Legacy Publishers International, 2004), 142.

6. Ibid., 144.

7. Ibid., 146–147.

8. Joni Eareckson Tada and Steven Estes, *When God Weeps: Why Our Sufferings Matter to the Almighty* (Grand Rapids, MI: Zondervan, 1997), 203.

Chapter 2 • What Does It Mean to Stand Strong?

1. Bob Sorge, *Unrelenting Prayer* (Kansas City, MO: Oasis House, 2005), 25–26.

2. Rick Renner, *Sparkling Gems From the Greek* (Tulsa, OK: Rick Renner Ministries, 2003), 157–158.

Chapter 3 • How to Walk in the Spirit

1. Watchman Nee, *Sit, Walk, Stand* (Fort Washington, PA: Christian Literature Crusade, 1969), 43.

2. Enoch's prophecy is not found in the canonical books of our Bible today. The prophecy, as well as the phrase "seventh generation from Adam," comes from "the noncanonical book of Enoch [which] contains portions that can be dated from the beginning of the Christian era" (*NRSV Harper Study Bible*, expanded edition [Grand Rapids, MI: Zondervan, 1991], note for Jude 14, page 1844).

3. Rod Parsley, *Daily Breakthrough* (Lake Mary, FL: Charisma House, 1998), 105.

4. Oswald Chambers, *My Utmost for His Highest: An Updated Edition in Today's Language*, ed. James Reimann (Nashville, TN: Discovery House, 1992), "The Teaching of Adversity," August 2.

CHAPTER 4 ◆ CONFIDENT IN YOUR CALLING

1. Chambers, *My Utmost For His Highest*, "Is This True of Me?" March 4.

2. Myles Munroe, *The Principles and Power of Vision: Keys to Achieving Personal and Corporate Destiny* (New Kensington, PA: Whitaker House, 2003), 47.

3. Chambers, *My Utmost for His Highest*, "The Bewildering Call of God," August 5; "The Voice of the Nature of God," January 16.

CHAPTER 5 ◆ STRONG IN ADVERSITY

1. John Foxe, *The New Foxe's Book of Martyrs*, ed. Harold J. Chadwick (Gainesville, FL: Bridge-Logos, 2001), 10.

2. Chambers, *My Utmost for His Highest*, "The Habit of Rising to the Occasion," May 15.

3. Finis Jennings Dake, ed., *Dake's Annotated Reference Bible* (Atlanta, GA: Dake Bible Sales, 1963), s.v. Isaiah 50:7, note a.

4. Ibid., s.v. Ezekiel 3:8–9, note i.

5. Parsley, *Daily Breakthrough*, 43.

CHAPTER 6 ◆ BALANCED WITH GODLY CHARACTER

1. Billy Graham Center Archives Staff, "Billy Graham and the Billy Graham Evangelistic Association—Historical Background," http://www.wheaton.edu/bgc/archives/bio.html (accessed April 4, 2006).

2. Harold Bloom, "Billy Graham," *TIME*, June 14, 1999, from online archives, http://www.time.com/time/time100/heroes/profile/graham01.html (accessed April 4, 2006).

3. David Aikman, *Great Souls: Six Who Changed the Century* (Nashville, TN: Word, 1998).

4. As quoted in Helen Kooiman Hosier, *100 Christian Women Who Changed the Twentieth Century* (Grand Rapids, MI: Fleming H. Revell, 2000), 77.

5. Joyce Meyer, *A Leader in the Making: Essentials to Being a Leader After God's Own Heart* (New York: Warner Books, 2002), 246.

6. R. T. Kendall, *The Anointing: Yesterday, Today, Tomorrow* (Lake Mary, FL: Charisma House, 2003), 19–20.

7. Smith Wigglesworth, "A Living Faith," *Triumphs of Faith* (Oakland, CA), January 1930, as quoted in *Only Believe! Selected Inspirational Readings*, Wayne E. Warner, ed. (Ann Arbor, MI: Servant, 1996), 26.

8. Meyer, *A Leader in the Making*, 63.

CHAPTER 7 ✦ VIOLENT IN YOUR FAITH

1. Francis Frangipane, *This Day We Fight! Breaking the Bondage of a Passive Spirit* (Grand Rapids, MI: Chosen, 2005), 112–113.

2. From *Triumphs of Faith* (Oakland, CA), May 1921, 113–114. Reprinted from *Confidence* (Sunderland, England) and collected in Wayne E. Warner and Joyce Lee, *The Essential Smith Wigglesworth: Selected Messages by the Legendary Evangelist From Powerful Revival Campaigns Around the World* (Ann Arbor, MI: Servant, 1999), 322.

3. "A Mighty Fortress Is Our God" by Martin Luther, trans. Frederick H. Hedge. Public domain.

4. Frangipane, *This Day We Fight!* 67.

CHAPTER 8 ✦ PERSISTENT IN YOUR PRAYER

1. Sorge, *Unrelenting Prayer*, 20–21.

2. AwakeandGo.com, "Awake and Go! Kingdom Quotes: Prayer, Revival, and Missions...," http://www.watchword.org//index.php?option=com_content&task=view&id=5&Itemid=23 (accessed February 13, 2007).

3. Beliefnet.com, Today's Bible Reading, "A Lion in the House of Judah," October 5, 2006, http://www.beliefnet.com/dailybible/1110506.htm (accessed February 13, 2007).

4. Sorge, *Unrelenting Prayer*, 152.

5. Tim Storey, *Good Idea or God-Idea?* (Lake Mary, FL: Charisma House, 1994).

6. Munroe, *Understanding the Purpose and Power of Prayer*, 106.

CHAPTER 9 ✦ CONSISTENT IN YOUR PRAISE AND WORSHIP

1. Joseph L. Garlington, *Worship: The Pattern of Things in Heaven* (Shippensburg, PA: Destiny Image, 1997), 5.

2. J. D. Douglas, ed., *The New Bible Dictionary* (Grand Rapids, MI: Eerdmans, 1962), 1018.

3. SearchGodsWord.org, Old/New Testament Greek, keyword praise, http://www.searchgodsword.org/lex/grk/ (accessed July 12, 2006).

CHAPTER 10 ✦ HAVING DONE ALL

1. Bob Sorge, *In His Face: A Prophetic Call to Renewed Focus* (Greenwood, MO: Oasis House, 1994), 24–25.

2. Sorge, *Unrelenting Prayer*, 16–17.

YOU CAN EMERGE TRIUMPHANT!

If you have been encouraged and challenged by Judy Jacobs in **Stand Strong**, here is another book, written in the same straightforward, gutsy, encouraging style, that we think you will enjoy:

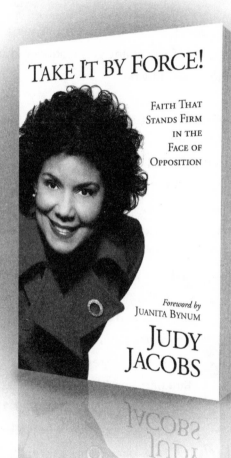